ice cream
and frozen desserts

ice cream
and frozen desserts

Peggy Fallon

DK Publishing

LONDON, NEW YORK, MELBOURNE, MUNICH, DELHI

This book is dedicated to JMG—always in my heart.

Editor Nichole Morford
Designer Bill Miller
Managing Art Editor Michelle Baxter
Art Director Dirk Kaufman
Executive Managing Editor Sharon Lucas
Publishing Director Carl Raymond
DTP Coordinator Kathy Farias
Production Manager Ivor Parker

Packaged by King Hill Productions
Food Stylist Alison Attenborough
Food photography by Ngoc Minh Ngo, unless noted below:
Author photo by Larry Guyer
Additional ingredient photography by Bill Miller (pages 29, 59, 77, 95, 97)

Published by DK Publishing, 375 Hudson Street, New York, NY 10014

07 08 09 10 10 9 8 7 6 5 4 3 2 1

Copyright © 2007 by DK Publishing
Text copyright © 2007 by King Hill Productions

A Catalog record for this book is available from the Library of Congress.
ISBN 978-0-7566-2885-7

Reproduced by Colourscan (Singapore)
Printed and bound in China by Leo Paper

Discover more at **www.dk.com**

Contents

Making Ice Cream at Home

What is America's hands-down absolutely all-time favorite dessert? Ice cream, of course. That pleasing jolt of sweet cold in the mouth, followed by the sensual richness of frozen cream and burst of flavor on the tongue, satisfies in a way few other desserts can. Sometimes there's the added delight of a crackle of nuts or chocolate bits or specks of candy. Perhaps a whiff of ethereal cream on top, a splash of a liqueur, or the warm, sludgy goodness of hot fudge sauce or warm caramel to transform the perfect dessert into an over-the-top sundae.

Of course, ice cream can be purchased almost anywhere, but there's a new twist in the frozen world of desserts: homemade. A generation of improved ice cream makers, freed from salt and ice, many of them with built-in compressors for convenient freezing, has made homemade ice cream making easier—and quicker—than ever.

Controlling the ingredients you feed to your family and involving children in the kitchen are just a couple of good reasons for making ice cream at home. Customizing your own flavors and controlling the fat content and level of sweetness are several more. Homemade also allows you to pick from a wide range of types of frozen desserts, from creamy to lean: rich ice creams, light ice creams, frozen yogurts, ice milk, gelato, sorbet, sherbets, and granita. Most of all, ice cream making is easy, and it's fun.

In this collection you'll find a range of flavors, from Almost-Instant Banana, Cinnamon-Basil, and Chocolate-Chipotle Ice Cream and Espresso Bean Gelato with Toffee Bits to Mango-Pineapple, Pomegranate Martini, and Green Apple Sorbet. Plus, there are over two dozen ideas for "almost-instant" recipes—sumptuous desserts quickly assembled from store-bought ingredients. There are recipes for sauces, toppings, and swirls, as well.

Ice cream also serves here as a ready-made base for any number of pies, cakes, and creative confections for entertaining. Frozen desserts take an enormous burden off the cook, because they must be prepared in advance. Name a child who wouldn't be delighted by a Chocolate Cookie Ice Cream Cake for her birthday? Or an adult whose eyes wouldn't light up at a Mile-High Lemon Chiffon Ice Cream Pie? Some of these fantasy creations are whimsical. Watermelon Bombe, which looks just like a big slice of fruit, Ice Cream Baked Potato, and Ice Cream Spaghetti are guaranteed to be the life of the party.

When making ice cream at home, there are several facts you should know. For one thing, unless you are using a professional machine that costs thousands of dollars, or an old-fashioned salt-and-ice bucket, no home ice cream maker freezes ice cream solid. Whether you are using a completely automatic machine or an ice cream maker that requires pre-freezing the canister overnight, the end product will be the same: a cohesive mass that is not solid. You could think of it as "soft serve." To transform this semi-frozen product into a proper frozen dessert, the ice cream that comes out of the machine must be transferred to a covered container and set in the freezer for several hours. This final freezing period improves texture and also allows the ice cream to cure and mellow, deepening its flavor.

About Ice Cream Makers

These days, there is an ice cream machine for every budget and every lifestyle. The purpose of any ice cream maker is to break up ice crystals as they form during the freezing process. This constant movement, called churning, also incorporates air to improve the texture and increase the volume of the finished ice cream. Since all types of machines make remarkably good ice cream, you must make your decision based upon convenience, capacity, and budget. As with many things in life, price is often an indicator of quality.

Automatic Ice Cream Machines with Built-In Compressors

Since the introduction of the Simac ice cream machine in the 1980s, the gelato-loving Italians have led the technology revolution. Models like Musso's *Lussino* and *Pola* operate like little Ferraris, though their price tags may make them out of reach for anyone other than the most serious ice cream maker. However, Lello has recently come out with a line called *Gelato Pro*, which comes in both 1½- and 2-quart (1½- and 2-liter) models and pairs top-notch performance with affordable price. The 2-quart, especially, is very quiet.

Cuisinart has also developed a machine that is both affordable and sleek. Although it's a little slower and noiser than some, it reliably churns out batch after batch of quality ice cream. Other brands like Deni, Nemox, Salton, and Whynter also meet the demand for affordable compressor-type ice cream makers. Look for new models and brands each season, as the technology continues to improve.

Frozen-Canister Ice Cream Makers

Several decades ago, Donvier introduced an inexpensive lightweight, hand-cranked maker based around a coolant-filled canister that was first frozen until solid. Now a number of different manufacturers offer electric models that make anywhere from 1 to 2 quarts (1 to 2 liters) of ice cream in about 30 minutes. Even KitchenAid makes a special freezer-ready bowl and dasher attachment that converts their stand mixer into an ice cream maker, with surprisingly good results. In order for any of these machines to work properly, the bulky canister must be kept in your freezer for a full 24 hours before using. On the other hand, the cost is quite reasonable.

Salt-and-Ice Ice Cream Churners

In this classic bucket-type machine from White Mountain, the canister is continually rotated by either hand-cranking or by electric power, depending upon the model. The freezing process is accomplished by surrounding the canister with layers of crushed or shaved ice and coarse rock salt, a mix that melts into an icy brine that lowers the temperature of the churning ice cream until it reaches its freezing point. The downside is that the ice-packing procedure is messy, so these are best used outdoors or inside a large waterproof tub to contain leaking brine. Perfect for parties, these machines freeze 4 to 6 quarts (4 to 6 liters) of ice cream in 25 to 35 minutes, but are not suited to making small batches.

Ingredient Guide

As with all good food, ingredients are everything in ice cream and other frozen desserts. Your dairy products and eggs should be pristinely fresh, organic if possible. This guide will direct you to the best ice-cream making ingredients available.

Chocolate: As a general rule, the higher the cacao content of chocolate, the greater the intensity of flavor. That's because cacao is pure chocolate. Both semisweet and bittersweet chocolate must contain a minimum of 35 percent cacao; many premium brands contain as much as 72 percent. Sugar is added for sweetness and cocoa butter for smoothness, along with a small amount of vanilla and soy lecithin as an emulsifier. Many of the better brands now list cacao content on their labels as a sign of quality, though the exact sweetness and bitterness of the finished chocolate is determined by the manufacturer. Unless a certain type of chocolate is specified in the recipe, semisweet and bittersweet can be used interchangeably, according to your taste preference. All chocolate should be melted over very low heat, stirring frequently.

Cocoa powder: Almost all the recipes in this book specify unsweetened Dutch process cocoa powder. Chocolate is naturally acidic, and this type of cocoa is treated to neutralize the acidity. This results in a darker cocoa with a mellower flavor.

Eggs: Use Grade AA "large" eggs, preferably organic, whenever a recipe calls for whole eggs or egg yolks. Extra-large eggs will not adversely affect the finished product; they'll just add a bit of extra richness. Jumbo, however, may throw off the formulas. When an ice cream calls for an egg custard base, you'll note it is cooked to 170° to 175°F (75° to 80°C). This ensures all bacteria are killed and thickens the yolks to the proper body needed for a silky, rich frozen cream. Do not let temperature rise above 180°F (85°C) or the egg yolks may curdle.

Flavor extracts: These must be pure, especially **vanilla**. Otherwise your ice cream will taste artificial and will lack the bright, clean taste of a natural product. **Liqueurs and spirits** are also used as flavorings, especially in sorbets. Since alcohol will never completely freeze, this addition also prevents the sorbet from freezing into a solid mass. Never double or triple the specified amount of alcohol: you'll end up with slush.

Fresh fruits: Fruits and berries should be perfectly ripe. Freezing dulls flavors, so to ensure the essence of a fruit shines through, use produce whose taste and aroma is at its peak.

Heavy cream: This is cream with a butterfat content of between 36 and 40 percent. The same cream is sometimes called "whipping cream" or "heavy whipping cream." Any of these can be used interchangeably. If possible, avoid cream labeled "ultra-pasteurized."

Milk: Use whole milk, unless otherwise specified. In most cases, two percent or nonfat milk will result in a frozen dessert that is too icy and will melt too quickly.

Nuts: As most bakers know, nuts are rich in oils that can quickly turn rancid, especially in warm weather. Buy your nuts in a sealed container or in bulk from a good source. Store them in a covered jar or sealed container in the refrigerator or freezer.

Plain yogurt: Plain means unflavored. Unless a recipe specifies to use low-fat, be sure to use a whole milk-based yogurt.

Salt: A pinch of salt brightens sweet flavors, especially when chocolate is involved.

Sugar: Use pure cane granulated sugar. In addition to its obvious role as a sweetener, sugar plays an important part in determining the texture of finished ice cream. Artificial sweeteners do not react the same; they produce an unpleasantly hard ice cream, which could possibly damage your machine.

Now that you've got the whole scoop, it's time to get started!

"without ice cream, there would be darkness and chaos."

–Don Kardong, 1976 U.S. Olympic marathoner

rich ice creams, frozen custards, & gelatos

tian Double Vanilla
Cream

If you love vanilla, why bother with an ice cream recipe that contains only a miserly teaspoon of the luscious essence? This version flaunts a double dose of fragrant vanilla, placing it right at the head of its class. Tahitian vanilla has a heady floral flavor, worth its extra price.

INGREDIENTS

1 vanilla bean, preferably Tahitian

3 cups heavy cream

1 cup milk

¾ cup sugar

Dash of salt

4 egg yolks

1 tablespoon Tahitian vanilla extract

Makes about 1 quart (1 liter)

1 Using the pointed tip of a sharp knife, split the vanilla bean in half lengthwise and scrape the tiny black seeds into a heavy medium saucepan. Add the vanilla bean, cream, and milk and bring to a simmer over medium heat. Remove from the heat, cover, and let stand at room temperature for 30 minutes to blend the flavors.

2 Add the sugar and salt. Return to medium heat and cook, stirring occasionally, until the sugar dissolves and the mixture is hot, about 5 minutes.

3 Beat the egg yolks lightly in a medium bowl. Gradually whisk in about 1 cup of the warm vanilla cream. Return the egg mixture to the saucepan, reduce the heat to medium-low, and cook, stirring, until the custard thickens enough to coat the back of a spoon, 170° to 175°F (75° to 80°C). Do not let boil, or the egg yolks will curdle.

4 Strain the custard into a bowl, pressing through as many of the vanilla seeds as you can. Refrigerate, covered, until the custard is very cold, at least 6 hours or as long as 2 days.

5 Stir in the vanilla extract. Pour the custard into the canister of an ice cream maker and freeze according to the manufacturer's directions. Transfer the ice cream to a covered container and freeze until it is firm enough to scoop, at least 3 hours or overnight.

Pistachio Gelato

Pistachio is an old-fashioned flavor that's been embraced by contemporary cuisine. Be sure to choose nuts that are fresh and have not been salted. Just a couple of drops of food coloring impart the familiar pale green of the nuts.

1 In a food processor, combine the pistachios with ¼ cup of the sugar. Pulse until the nuts are finely chopped; take care not to process to a paste.

2 In a heavy medium saucepan, combine the chopped pistachios and the milk. Bring to a simmer over medium heat. Remove from the heat, cover, and let steep at room temperature for 30 minutes to allow the flavor to develop.

3 Stir in the remaining ½ cup sugar and the salt. Return to medium heat and cook, stirring occasionally, until the sugar dissolves and the mixture is hot, about 5 minutes.

4 Beat the egg yolks lightly in a medium bowl. Gradually whisk in about 1 cup of the warm pistachio milk. Whisk the egg mixture into the remaining pistachio milk in the saucepan, reduce the heat to medium-low, and cook, stirring, until the custard thickens enough to coat the back of a spoon, 170° to 175°F (75° to 80°C). Do not let boil, or the egg yolks will curdle.

5 Strain the custard into a bowl; discard the nuts. Whisk in the food coloring. Cover and refrigerate for 4 hours, or until the custard is very cold. Stir in the almond extract.

6 Pour the custard into the canister of an ice cream maker and freeze according to the manufacturer's directions. Transfer the gelato to a covered container and freeze until it is firm enough to scoop, at least 3 hours or overnight.

INGREDIENTS

1 cup unsalted shelled pistachio nuts

¾ cup sugar

2 cups whole milk

Dash of salt

5 egg yolks

2 drops of green food coloring

1 teaspoon almond extract

Makes about 1 quart (1 liter)

COOL TIPS FOR SUCCESS

Use a candy thermometer or instant-read thermometer to measure the exact temperature of your cooked custard. At 170° to 175°F (75° to 80°C), the mixture will be thick enough to coat a spoon and will freeze into a silky, smooth ice cream.

Fresh Peach Ice Cream

Nothing speaks of high summer more than fresh ripe peaches, and this ice cream offers a great way to use them. To peel peaches, slip them into a pot of boiling water for 15 to 20 seconds, then rinse under cold water. The skins will slip right off.

1 In a food processor, pulse the peaches to chop them coarsely. Add ¼ cup of the sugar and the lemon juice and pulse 2 or 3 times to mix. Do not overprocess to a puree. Transfer to a bowl and let macerate at room temperature for 1 hour.

2 In a heavy medium saucepan, combine the cream and milk. Bring to a simmer over medium heat. Stir in the remaining ½ cup sugar and the salt and cook, stirring occasionally, until the sugar dissolves and the mixture is hot, about 5 minutes.

3 Beat the egg yolks lightly in a medium bowl. Gradually whisk in about 1 cup of the warm cream. Return the egg mixture to the saucepan, reduce the heat to medium-low, and cook, stirring, until the custard thickens enough to coat the back of a spoon, 170° to 175°F (75° to 80°C). Do not let boil, or the egg yolks will curdle.

4 Strain the custard into a bowl and stir in the chopped peaches with all their juices. Refrigerate, covered, until the custard is very cold, at least 6 hours or as long as 2 days. Stir in the almond extract.

5 Pour the custard into the canister of an ice cream maker and freeze according to the manufacturer's directions. Transfer the ice cream to a covered container and freeze until it is firm enough to scoop, at least 3 hours or overnight.

INGREDIENTS

1 pound (450 grams) ripe peaches, peeled and pitted

¾ cup sugar

½ teaspoon fresh lemon juice

3 cups heavy cream

1 cup milk

Dash of salt

4 egg yolks

1 teaspoon almond extract or vanilla extract

Makes about 1 quart (1 liter)

Meyer Lemon
and Mascarpone Ice Cream

Meyer lemons are a less acidic variety. They are common in California, seasonal on the East Coast. If making this with ordinary lemons, use ⅓ cup lemon juice and 3 tablespoons tangerine or orange juice.

1 Preheat the oven to 325°F (160°C). Spread out the almonds on a small baking sheet. Toast in the oven for 7 to 10 minutes, until the nuts are fragrant and golden. Let cool slightly, then coarsely chop.

2 Grate the zest from 2 of the lemons into a small bowl. Squeeze enough lemons to yield ½ cup lemon juice. Add to the zest.

3 In a heavy nonreactive medium saucepan, warm the cream and milk over medium heat until tiny bubbles form around the edges of the pan. Remove from the heat.

4 Beat the egg yolks lightly. Whisk in the sugar and beat until well blended and pale yellow. Gradually whisk in about 1 cup of the warm cream. Slowly whisk the egg yolk mixture into the remaining cream in the saucepan. Cook over medium-low heat, stirring, until the custard thickens enough to coat the back of a spoon, 170° to 175°F (75° to 80°C). Do not let boil, or the egg yolks will curdle.

5 Strain the custard through a fine sieve into a bowl. Let cool for 10 minutes. Whisk in the mascarpone until well blended. Mix in the lemon zest and juice and the vanilla. Cover and refrigerate until chilled.

6 Pour the lemon custard into the canister of an ice cream maker and freeze according to the manufacturer's directions. Add the chopped toasted almonds and process for 1 minute longer. Transfer the ice cream to a covered container and freeze until it is firm enough to scoop, at least 3 hours or overnight.

INGREDIENTS

⅓ cup slivered almonds
4 large Meyer lemons
1 cup heavy cream
1 cup whole milk
4 egg yolks
¾ cup sugar
1 cup (8-ounce or 225-gram) mascarpone
1 teaspoon vanilla extract

Makes about 1 quart (1 liter)

Lemon-Nutmeg Frozen Custard

What looks like a lot of nutmeg mellows surprisingly when frozen. This unusual ice cream proves that freshly grated nutmeg is destined for greater things than the finishing touch on eggnog. When paired with tart lemons and fragrant vanilla, the result is ethereal.

1 Using the pointed tip of a small knife, split the vanilla bean in half lengthwise and scrape the tiny black seeds into a heavy medium saucepan. Add the half-and-half and bring to a simmer over medium heat. Remove from the heat, cover, and let stand at room temperature for 30 minutes to blend the flavors.

2 In a large bowl, whisk together the sugar and egg yolks until well blended. Gradually whisk in about 1 cup of the warm half-and-half. Return the egg mixture to the saucepan, reduce the heat to medium-low, and cook, stirring, until the custard thickens enough to coat the back of a spoon, 170° to 175°F (75° to 80°C). Do not let boil, or the egg yolks will curdle.

3 Strain the custard into a bowl, pressing through as many of the vanilla seeds as you can. Cover and refrigerate for at least 3 hours, or until the custard is very cold.

4 Stir in the lemon zest, lemon juice, and grated nutmeg. Pour the custard into the canister of an ice cream maker and freeze according to the manufacturer's directions. Transfer to a covered container and freeze until it is firm enough to scoop, at least 3 hours or overnight.

INGREDIENTS

1 vanilla bean, split in half

4 cups half-and-half

2 cups sugar

6 egg yolks

1 tablespoon grated lemon zest

½ cup fresh lemon juice (3 or 4 lemons)

1 tablespoon freshly grated nutmeg

Makes about 5 cups

COOL TIPS FOR SUCCESS

To avoid curdling in ice creams that are custard-based, the egg yolks are first "tempered": some of the hot milk or cream is slowly whisked into the yolks to warm them gently before whisking them into the rest of the hot liquid.

Cinnamon-Basil Ice Cream

Chef Jerry Traunfeld of The Herbfarm restaurant outside of Seattle created this enchanting flavor of ice cream. If you have a garden and grow cinnamon basil, by all means use it here. Serve with a light dusting of cinnamon, if you like.

1 Bring the milk to a simmer in a heavy medium saucepan over medium heat. Add the basil and cinnamon stick, cover, and remove from the heat. Let steep for 15 minutes, then strain through a sieve, pressing down on the basil to extract all the liquid.

2 Whisk together the egg yolks and sugar in a large mixing bowl. Slowly whisk in the cinnamon-basil flavored milk. Return to the saucepan and cook over medium heat, stirring constantly with a silicone spatula or wooden spoon, until the custard thickens enough to coat the back of a spoon, 170° to 175°F (75° to 80°C). Do not let boil, or the egg yolks will curdle.

3 Immediately pour the custard back into the mixing bowl and let cool, either over a larger bowl of ice with a little water or in the refrigerator, until the custard is very cold. Whisk in the heavy cream.

4 Pour the base into the canister of an ice cream maker and freeze according to the manufacturer's directions. Transfer the ice cream to a covered container and freeze until it is firm enough to scoop, at least 3 hours or overnight.

INGREDIENTS

2½ cups milk

1 bunch (about 1 ounce or 25 grams) of fresh basil, well-rinsed

1 cinnamon stick

8 egg yolks

1 cup sugar

1½ cups heavy cream

Makes about 1½ quarts (1½ liters)

lost-Instant
~~nana Ice Cream

Sweetened condensed milk, half-and-half, and heavy cream combine to make a lush ice cream that needs no cooked custard. Since only the condensed milk needs chilling here, your base should be ready in an hour or less. For best flavor, be sure the bananas are very ripe, nicely speckled with brown spots.

1 In a large bowl, whisk together the half-and-half, sweetened condensed milk, heavy cream, and vanilla until well blended. Cover and refrigerate for 1 hour, or until cold.

2 Pour into the canister of an ice cream maker and freeze according to the manufacturer's directions until the ice cream is softly frozen.

3 Mash the bananas with the lemon juice. Add to the ice cream maker and continue to process for 2 minutes longer. Transfer the ice cream to a covered container and freeze until it is firm enough to scoop, at least 3 hours or overnight.

INGREDIENTS

2   cups half-and-half
1   can (14 ounces or 400 grams) sweetened condensed milk
1   cup heavy cream
1   teaspoon vanilla extract
2   very ripe bananas
2   teaspoons fresh lemon or lime juice

Makes about 1 quart (1 liter)

VARIATION

Almost-Instant Strawberry Ice Cream: Substitute 1 cup crushed strawberries for the bananas.

Butter Pecan Ice Cream

There really is butter in this sumptuous ice cream, which gives it extra richness and body. If you can find fresh southern pecans, their sweetness and flavor will really stand out here.

INGREDIENTS

1   cup pecan halves and pieces

2   cups whole milk

1   cup heavy cream

⅔   cup granulated sugar

¼   cup (packed) dark brown sugar

6   tablespoons unsalted butter, cut into pieces

4   egg yolks

1   teaspoon vanilla extract

¼   teaspoon salt

Makes about 1 quart (1 liter)

1   Preheat the oven to 325°F (160°C). Spread out the pecans in a baking pan and bake for 7 to 10 minutes, or until lightly toasted and fragrant. Set aside to cool.

2   In a heavy medium saucepan, combine the milk, cream, granulated sugar, and brown sugar. Cook over medium heat, stirring occasionally for about 5 minutes, until the sugars dissolve and the mixture is hot.

3   In a heavy small saucepan, cook the butter over medium heat, stirring occasionally, until very lightly browned. Remove from the heat but keep warm.

4   Beat the egg yolks with the salt lightly in a medium bowl. Gradually whisk the browned butter and then about 1 cup of the warm cream into the yolks. Return the egg mixture to the saucepan, reduce the heat to medium-low, and cook, stirring, until the custard thickens enough to coat the back of a spoon, 170° to 175°F (75° to 80°C). Do not let boil, or the egg yolks will curdle.

5   Strain the custard into a bowl. Cover and refrigerate until the custard is very cold, at least 6 hours or as long as 2 days. Whisk in the vanilla.

6   Pour into the canister of an ice cream maker and freeze according to the manufacturer's directions. Add the pecans and process for 1 minute longer. Transfer the ice cream to a covered container and freeze until it is firm enough to scoop, 3 hours or overnight.

Eggnog Ice Cream with Hot Buttered Rum Sauce

Dust off that old punch bowl and serve scoops of this spiked ice cream in little cups, drizzled with Hot Buttered Rum Sauce and garnished with a dollop of whipped cream and a grating of fresh nutmeg. Because the flavor is as rich as you expect eggnog to be, servings should be small.

1 In a heavy medium saucepan, combine the milk, cream, and sugar. Cook over medium heat, stirring occasionally, until the sugar dissolves and the mixture is hot, about 5 minutes.

2 Beat the egg yolks lightly in a medium bowl. Gradually whisk in about 1 cup of the hot cream. Gradually whisk this egg yolk mixture into the remaining cream mixture in the saucepan. Reduce the heat to medium-low, and cook, stirring, until the custard thickens enough to coat the back of a spoon, 170° to 175°F (75° to 80°C). Do not let boil, or the egg yolks will curdle.

3 Strain the custard into a bowl and stir in the rum. Cover and refrigerate until the custard is very cold, at least 6 hours or as long as 2 days. Stir in the vanilla and nutmeg.

4 Pour the custard into the canister of an ice cream maker and freeze according to the manufacturer's directions. Transfer the ice cream to a covered container and freeze until it is firm enough to scoop, at least 3 hours or overnight. Drizzle Hot Buttered Rum Sauce over each serving and dust with a pinch of grated nutmeg.

Hot Buttered Rum Sauce

In a small saucepan, melt the butter over medium heat. Whisk in the brown sugar, cream, corn syrup, and salt. Bring to a boil and cook for 1 minute. Remove from the heat and stir in the rum. Use at once, or cover and refrigerate for up to 2 days.

INGREDIENTS

2   cups whole milk
1½ cups heavy cream
⅔   cup sugar
4   egg yolks
3   tablespoons dark rum, such as Myers's
1   teaspoon vanilla extract
¼   teaspoon freshly grated nutmeg

Makes about 1 quart (1 liter)

Hot Buttered Rum Sauce
1   stick (4 ounces or 100 grams) unsalted butter, cut into pieces
1   cup (packed) light brown sugar
½   cup heavy cream
2   tablespoons light corn syrup
Dash of salt
2   tablespoons dark rum, such as Myers's

Makes about 1½ cups

Rum-Raisin Pumpkin Ice Cream

Unsweetened canned pumpkin for pies is the only kind to use for this special recipe. It's made from a variety of squash that yields exactly the right taste for this sweetly spiced dessert. Fresh pumpkin will not be intense enough. Serve the ice cream by itself or over a slice of pound cake or gingerbread.

1 In a nonreactive small saucepan, combine the raisins and rum. Bring to a bare simmer over low heat. (Watch carefully, adjusting the heat as needed; if the alcohol gets too hot, it can ignite.) Remove from the heat and let cool.

2 In a large bowl, gradually whisk the sugar into the cream until it dissolves. Whisk in the pumpkin, ginger, cinnamon, and cloves. Cover and refrigerate until cold, at least 2 hours or as long as 2 days.

3 Whisk the ice cream base to blend. Pour into the canister of an ice cream maker and freeze according to the manufacturer's directions. Add the raisins along with any remaining rum and process for 1 minute longer. Transfer the ice cream to a covered container and freeze until it is firm enough to scoop, at least 3 hours or overnight.

INGREDIENTS

¾ cup dark raisins
    (about 6 ounces or 175 grams)

½ cup dark rum,
    such as Myers's

2 cups sugar

2 cups heavy cream

1 can (about 15 ounces or 425 grams) solid-pack unsweetened pumpkin

¼ teaspoon ground ginger

¼ teaspoon ground cinnamon

¼ teaspoon ground cloves

Makes about 1 quart (1 liter)

No-Cook Vanilla Ice Cream

In a hurry? Here's the recipe to turn to. Since there is no cooking, no eggs, and all the ingredients are cold to begin with, you can make homemade ice cream in less than half an hour, if your machine is up to it. The texture is a bit icier than custard-based ice creams, so the dessert is best served the same day it is made, but there is a lot to be said for instant gratification.

1 In a large bowl, combine the milk, cream, and salt. Gradually whisk in the sugar and vanilla. If you have time, cover and refrigerate for 1 to 2 hours to allow the flavors to develop.

2 Pour into the canister of an ice cream maker and freeze according to the manufacturer's directions. Transfer the ice cream to a covered container and freeze until it is firm enough to scoop, at least 3 hours or overnight.

INGREDIENTS

1½ cups whole milk

1½ cups heavy cream

Dash of salt

⅔ cup sugar

2 teaspoons vanilla extract

Makes about 1 quart (1 liter)

VARIATION

No-Cook Chocolate Cookie Swirl Ice Cream: Prepare the No-Cook Vanilla Ice Cream above. After the ice cream is frozen according to the manufacturer's directions, with the machine on, add ¾ cup coarsely crushed creme-filled chocolate sandwich cookies, such as Oreos®, or chocolate wafer cookies and process for 30 to 60 seconds, until just swirled through. Transfer to a covered container and freeze for at least 3 hours before serving.

White Chocolate Ice Cream
with Bittersweet Fudge Ripple

When shopping for white chocolate, be sure to choose pure white chocolate and not confectionery or summer coating. Cocoa butter should be listed as the primary ingredient on the label. To make plain white chocolate ice cream, simply omit the fudge swirl.

1 In a heavy nonreactive medium saucepan, combine the milk, cream, sugar, and salt. Bring to a simmer over medium heat, stirring, until the sugar dissolves and the mixture is hot, about 5 minutes. Remove from the heat. Add the chopped white chocolate and whisk until melted and smooth.

2 Beat the egg yolks lightly in a medium bowl. Gradually whisk in about 1 cup of the warm white chocolate cream. Gradually whisk the egg yolk–white chocolate mixture into the remaining cream in the pan. Reduce the heat to medium-low and cook, stirring, until the custard thickens enough to coat the back of a spoon, 170° to 175°F (75° to 80°C). Do not let boil, or the egg yolks will curdle.

3 Strain the custard into a bowl. Let cool slightly, then cover and refrigerate until the custard is very cold, at least 6 hours or as long as 2 days. Stir in the vanilla.

4 Pour the custard into the canister of an ice cream maker and freeze according to the manufacturer's directions. With the machine on, pour in the Bittersweet Fudge Sauce and process for 30 to 60 seconds, or until incorporated. Transfer the ice cream to a covered container and freeze until it is firm enough to scoop, at least 3 hours or overnight.

INGREDIENTS

1½ cups whole milk

1   cup heavy cream

½   cup sugar

Dash of salt

4   ounces (100 grams) white chocolate, finely chopped

4   egg yolks

½   teaspoon vanilla extract

1   cup Bittersweet Fudge Sauce (page 184)

Makes about 1 quart (1 liter)

Coconut Ice Cream
with Crystallized Ginger

Cool and refreshing, with a pleasant touch of heat from ginger, this ice cream is the perfect ending to any Asian-inspired or spicy meal. Serve plain or showered with toasted coconut.

1 Pour the coconut milk into a heavy medium saucepan, making sure to scrape in the thick part at the bottom; whisk to homogenize. Whisk in the cream, sugar, and salt. Cook over medium heat, stirring occasionally, for 5 minutes, or until the sugar dissolves and the coconut cream is hot.

2 Beat the egg yolks lightly in a medium bowl. Gradually whisk in about 1 cup of the warm coconut cream. Return the egg yolk mixture to the saucepan, reduce the heat to medium-low, and cook, stirring, until the custard thickens enough to coat the back of a spoon, 170° to 175°F (75° to 80°C). Do not let boil, or the egg yolks will curdle.

3 Strain the coconut custard into a bowl and let cool to room temperature. Cover and refrigerate until very cold, at least 6 hours or as long as 2 days.

4 Stir the ginger and vanilla into the coconut custard. Pour the custard into the canister of an ice cream maker and freeze according to the manufacturer's directions. Transfer the ice cream to a covered container and freeze until it is firm enough to scoop, at least 3 hours or overnight.

INGREDIENTS

1	can (13 to 14 ounces or 375 to 400 grams) unsweetened coconut milk
1	cup heavy cream
½	cup sugar
¼	teaspoon salt
3	egg yolks
3	tablespoons coarsely chopped crystallized ginger
1	teaspoon vanilla extract

Makes about 1 quart (1 liter)

COOL TIPS FOR SUCCESS

Straining the cooked custard through a sieve ensures that no chewy bits of cooked egg will ruin the texture of your ice cream.

Green Tea Ice Cream

Green tea powder, which is called *matcha*, can be found in the international food section of some supermarkets and in Asian markets and health food stores. It has a slightly smoky herbal taste with just a hint of bitterness and is a great antioxidant. As an ice cream, it's a good choice after a Chinese or Japanese meal, or when you want a subtle dessert that takes a back seat to the other courses.

1 In a large bowl, combine the milk and sugar. Whisk to dissolve the sugar. Whisk in the cream and salt.

2 Gradually whisk in the green tea powder 1 tablespoon at a time, blending until smooth. Stir in the vanilla. Cover and refrigerate for 1 to 2 hours to allow the flavors to develop.

3 Pour into the canister of an ice cream maker and freeze according to the manufacturer's directions. Transfer the ice cream to a covered container and freeze until it is firm enough to scoop, at least 3 hours or overnight.

INGREDIENTS

1   cup milk

¾   cup sugar

2   cups heavy cream

Dash of salt

3   tablespoons green tea powder (matcha)

⅛   teaspoon vanilla extract

Makes about 1 quart (1 liter)

Chocolate Custard Ice Cream

Rich, dark, silky, and smooth—this is everything chocolate ice cream should be. Because it calls for the best cocoa and chocolate, it's not too sweet.

INGREDIENTS

2½ cups whole milk

1   cup heavy cream

¾   cup sugar

Dash of salt

¼   cup Dutch process
     unsweetened
     cocoa powder

4   ounces (100 grams)
     bittersweet or semisweet
     chocolate, finely chopped

4   egg yolks

1½ teaspoons vanilla extract

Makes about 1 quart (1 liter)

1 In a heavy medium saucepan, combine the milk, cream, sugar, and salt. Bring to a simmer over medium heat, stirring, for about 5 minutes, or until the sugar dissolves and the mixture is hot. Remove from the heat and whisk in the cocoa powder until well blended. Whisk in the chopped chocolate until melted and smooth.

2 Beat the egg yolks lightly in a medium bowl. Gradually whisk in about 1 cup of the warm chocolate cream. Whisk the egg mixture into the remaining chocolate cream in the pan, reduce the heat to medium-low, and cook, stirring, until the custard thickens enough to coat the back of a spoon, 170° to 175°F (75° to 80°C). Do not let boil, or the egg yolks will curdle. Strain the chocolate custard into a bowl. Cover and refrigerate until the custard is very cold, at least 6 hours or as long as 2 days.

3 Stir in the vanilla. Pour the custard into the canister of an ice cream maker and freeze according to the manufacturer's directions. Transfer the ice cream to a covered container and freeze until firm enough to scoop, at least 3 hours or overnight.

VARIATION

Chocolate Custard Ice Cream with Marshmallow Swirl (pictured at right): Follow the recipe above, freezing the ice cream according to the manufacturer's directions. With the machine running, add half a 7-ounce (200-gram) jar of marshmallow cream, one heaping spoonful at a time, processing for 30 to 60 seconds, or until just swirled through. Transfer the ice cream to a covered container and freeze until firm enough to scoop, at least 3 hours.

Coffee Ice Cream

This recipe comes from Christine Law, and was perfected during her nine years as executive pastry chef for Wolfgang Puck's Spago and Postrio restaurants. Excellent scooped up on its own, no one will object to a drizzle of chocolate sauce and an extra splash of Kahlúa.

1 Place the coffee beans in a plastic bag and crush with a rolling pin; do not grind the beans in a coffee mill. Combine the crushed coffee beans, cream, whole milk, and evaporated milk in a heavy medium saucepan. Warm over medium-low heat until barely simmering. Remove from the heat, cover, and let steep for 30 minutes. Strain through a sieve lined with layers of cheesecloth.

2 Pour the coffee cream into a clean saucepan and stir in ⅓ cup of the sugar. Return to medium-low heat and cook, stirring to dissolve the sugar, until barely simmering.

3 In a large bowl with an electric mixer, beat the egg yolks with the corn syrup and remaining ⅓ cup sugar until fluffy. Slowly pour in 1 cup of the hot coffee cream in a thin stream. Whisk the egg yolk mixture into the remaining coffee cream. Cook over medium heat, whisking vigorously, until the temperature reaches 170° to 175°F (75° to 80°C). Do not boil, or the egg yolks will curdle.

4 Immediately strain through a fine sieve into a heatproof bowl.

5 Set the bowl over a larger bowl filled with ice and a little water and whisk occasionally until cooled to lukewarm. Blend in the Kahlúa, cover, and refrigerate for at least 4 hours or overnight.

6 Pour the coffee base into the canister of an ice cream maker and freeze according to the manufacturer's directions. Transfer to a covered container and freeze at least 3 hours or overnight.

INGREDIENTS

¼ cup French roast whole coffee beans

1½ cups heavy cream

1 cup whole milk

¼ cup evaporated skim milk

⅔ cup granulated sugar

4 egg yolks

1 tablespoon light corn syrup

2 teaspoons Kahlúa or 1 teaspoon coffee extract

Makes about 1½ pints (675 ml)

Mint Chocolate Chunk Ice Cream

An infusion of fresh mint imparts a subtle yet distinctive flavor to this delectable ice cream. It's much more sophisticated than commercial brands pumped up with artificial flavor. Because we're so used to green mint ice cream, you can add a few drops of green food coloring, but it's optional.

1 In a heavy nonreactive medium saucepan, combine the half-and-half, cream, mint, and lemon zest. Bring to a simmer over medium heat. Remove from the heat, cover, and let stand at room temperature for 30 minutes to allow the flavors to steep. Add the sugar and salt. Return to medium heat and cook, stirring occasionally, until the sugar dissolves and the liquid is hot, about 5 minutes.

2 Beat the egg yolks lightly in a medium bowl. Gradually whisk in about 1 cup of the warm mint cream. Whisk the egg yolk mixture into the mint cream remaining in the pan, reduce the heat to medium-low, and cook, stirring, until the custard thickens enough to coat the back of a spoon, 170° to 175°F (75° to 80°C). Do not let boil, or the egg yolks will curdle.

3 Strain the custard into a bowl, pressing on the mint with the back of a spoon to release the flavor; then discard the mint and lemon zest. Stir in the food coloring if you are using it. Cover and refrigerate until the custard is very cold, at least 6 hours.

4 Pour the custard into the canister of an ice cream maker and freeze according to the manufacturer's directions. Add the chocolate chunks and process for about 1 minute, until incorporated. Transfer the ice cream to a covered container and freeze until firm enough to scoop, at least 3 hours or overnight.

INGREDIENTS

3   cups half-and-half

1   cup heavy cream

1   cup (packed) fresh mint sprigs, preferably peppermint, coarsely chopped stems and all

1   thin strip of lemon zest, about 2 inches (5 cm) long and ½ inch (1¼ cm) wide

¾   cup sugar

Dash of salt

4   egg yolks

1 or 2 drops of green food coloring (optional)

4   ounces (100 grams) semisweet or mint-flavored chocolate chunks

Makes about 1 quart (1 liter)

COOL TIPS FOR SUCCESS

When you chop chocolate even coarsely, tiny powder bits flake off. To avoid small specks of chocolate in the finished ice cream, place the chopped chocolate in a sieve and shake to remove any fine bits. Save the chocolate powder for the next time you are melting chocolate or making hot chocolate.

Gianduja Chocolate Chunk Gelato

Gianduja combines chocolate with hazelnuts. You can buy bottles of hazelnut syrup at coffee bars and in many supermarkets. For an extra fillip, sprinkle chopped gianduja or dark chocolate and toasted hazelnuts over each serving.

1 Preheat the oven to 325°F (160°C). Toast the hazelnuts on a baking sheet for 10 to 12 minutes, until the nuts are lightly browned and fragrant. Rub the warm nuts in a towel to remove as much of the skin as possible. When cool, coarsely chop the nuts.

2 In a heavy medium saucepan, combine the milk and cream. Bring to a simmer over medium heat. Stir in the chopped hazelnuts and remove from the heat. Cover and let stand at room temperature for 30 minutes to cool and allow the flavors to develop. Strain to remove the nuts and return the hazelnut milk to the saucepan.

3 In a large bowl, whisk together the egg yolks, sugar, and salt until well blended. Whisk 1 cup of the warm hazelnut milk into the egg yolks. Whisk the egg yolk mixture into the remaining hazelnut milk in the saucepan. Cook over medium-low heat, stirring, until the custard thickens enough to coat the back of a spoon, 170° to 175°F (75° to 80°C). Do not let boil, or the egg yolks will curdle.

4 Strain the custard into a clean bowl. Add the unsweetened chocolate and whisk until melted and smooth. Stir in the hazelnut liqueur. Refrigerate, covered, until the custard is very cold, at least 6 hours or as long as 2 days.

5 Stir in the vanilla. Pour the custard into the canister of an ice cream maker and freeze according to the manufacturer's directions. Add the cold chocolate chunks and process for 1 minute longer. Transfer the gelato to a covered container and freeze until it is firm enough to scoop, 3 hours or overnight.

INGREDIENTS

1   cup hazelnuts (filberts)

2¼ cups whole milk

⅓   cup heavy cream

4   egg yolks

⅔   cup sugar

Dash of salt

2   ounces (50 grams) unsweetened chocolate, finely chopped

1   tablespoon hazelnut liqueur, such as Frangelico®, or hazelnut syrup

½   teaspoon vanilla extract

1   chocolate-hazelnut bar (3 to 4 ounces, or 75 to 100 grams) or other gianduja, chopped into small chunks and then refrigerated until cold

Makes about 1 quart (1 liter)

Chocolate-Chipotle Ice Cream

Creative cooks know that sweet and hot complement each other, and the Aztecs in Mexico long ago discovered how well fiery chiles and chocolate went together. Add a third element—cold—and you've got an irresistible as well as interesting flavor. Chipotles are smoked jalapeño chile peppers. They are sold in several forms—canned in adobo sauce, whole dried chiles, or ground into chile powder, as used in this recipe.

1 In a heavy medium saucepan, combine the cream, milk, sugar, and salt. Bring to a simmer over medium heat, stirring, for about 5 minutes, or until the sugar dissolves and the mixture is hot.

2 Remove from the heat and whisk in the chile powder and cinnamon. Add the chopped chocolate and whisk until melted and smooth. Cover and refrigerate for 3 hours, or until cold. Stir in the vanilla.

3 Pour into the canister of an ice cream maker and freeze according to the manufacturer's directions. Transfer the ice cream to a covered container and freeze until it is firm enough to scoop, at least 3 hours or overnight.

INGREDIENTS

2 cups heavy cream

1 cup whole milk

⅔ cup sugar

Dash of salt

1 teaspoon chipotle chile powder

½ teaspoon ground cinnamon

8 ounces (225 grams) semisweet chocolate, finely chopped

1 teaspoon vanilla extract

Makes about 1 quart (1 liter)

Espresso Bean Gelato with Toffee Bits

Espresso beans are simply coffee beans that have been darkly roasted. As with other coffee, the quality greatly affects the final flavor, so choose beans that are glossy and fragrant for this rich, silky ice cream.

1 Place the espresso beans in a heavy-duty zippered plastic bag. Coarsely crush with a rolling pin or under a heavy pot. Do not grind in a coffee mill.

2 In a heavy medium saucepan, combine the crushed espresso beans with the milk and cream. Bring to a simmer over medium heat. Remove from the heat, cover, and let steep at room temperature for 30 minutes.

3 Stir in the sugar and salt. Return to medium heat and cook, stirring occasionally, until the sugar dissolves and the mixture is hot, about 5 minutes.

4 Beat the egg yolks lightly in a medium bowl. Gradually whisk in about 1 cup of the warm espresso cream. Whisk the egg yolk mixture into the remaining espresso cream in the saucepan, reduce the heat to medium-low, and cook, stirring, until the custard thickens enough to coat the back of a spoon, 170° to 175°F (75° to 80°C). Do not let boil, or the egg yolks will curdle. Strain the custard into a bowl. Cover and refrigerate for 4 hours, or until very cold. Stir in the vanilla.

5 Pour the custard into the canister of an ice cream maker and freeze according to the manufacturer's directions. Add the chilled toffee candy and process for 1 minute longer, or until incorporated. Transfer the gelato to a covered container and freeze until it is firm enough to scoop, at least 3 hours or overnight.

INGREDIENTS

½ cup espresso coffee beans

2½ cups whole milk

½ cup heavy cream

¾ cup sugar

Dash of salt

6 egg yolks

1½ teaspoons vanilla extract

½ cup crushed chocolate-covered toffee candy, chilled, or crumbled biscotti

Makes about 1 quart (1 liter)

"it's amazing how quickly you recover from misery when someone offers you ice cream."

–Neil Simon, *Brighton Beach Memoirs*

light ice creams,
ice milks,
& sherbets

Quick Caramel-Pecan Light Ice Cream

With a jar of caramel sauce in your pantry and a package of chopped pecans, you've got all the makings you need for a delectable ice cream that requires no custard. The sticky caramel adds all the body that's needed for a rich and creamy dessert.

1 Preheat the oven to 325°F (160°C). Spread out the pecans in a baking pan and bake for 7 to 10 minutes, or until lightly toasted and fragrant. Transfer to a plate and set aside to cool.

2 In a large bowl, combine the half-and-half, caramel topping, vanilla, and salt. Whisk to blend. Cover and refrigerate for 2 hours, or until very cold.

3 Pour into the canister of an ice cream maker and freeze according to the manufacturer's directions. Add the pecans and process for 1 minute longer, or until incorporated. Transfer the ice cream to a covered container and freeze until it is firm enough to scoop, at least 3 hours or overnight.

INGREDIENTS

¾ cup coarsely chopped pecans

4 cups half-and-half

1 jar (10 ounces or 275 grams) caramel topping

2 teaspoons vanilla extract

Dash of salt

Makes about 1½ quarts (1½ liters)

Maple Walnut Light Ice Cream

Most maple walnut ice creams are custard based and exceptionally rich. But take the same excellent ingredients—Grade A amber maple syrup, fresh nuts, and pure vanilla—combine them with half-and-half instead of heavy cream, omit the egg yolks, and you've got a delightful dessert with half the fat.

1 Preheat the oven to 350°F (180°C). Spread out the walnuts on a baking sheet. Toast in the oven, stirring once or twice, for 8 to 10 minutes or until lightly browned and fragrant. Set aside to cool.

2 In a large bowl, combine the half-and-half, maple syrup, vanilla, and salt. If you have time, refrigerate for 1 to 2 hours to allow the flavors to develop.

3 Pour into the canister of an ice cream maker and freeze according to the manufacturer's directions. Add the walnuts and process for 1 minute longer, or until incorporated. Transfer the ice cream to a covered container and freeze until it is firm enough to scoop, at least 3 hours or overnight.

INGREDIENTS

1 cup coarsely chopped walnuts

3¼ cups half-and-half

1 cup pure maple syrup

1 teaspoon vanilla extract

Dash of salt

Makes about 1½ quarts (1½ liters)

COOL TIPS FOR SUCCESS

Fill your ice cream machine no fuller than the manufacturer recommends. Some air will be incorporated during the freezing process, and the ice cream needs room to expand. This aeration process, called overrun, improves the texture of the ice cream.

Lavender Ice Milk

It's only recently that cooks have realized lavender's potential for adding an evocative floral note to many preparations. In a funny way, it's a flavor that's both trendy and timelessly classical. To release lavender's essential oils, crush the dried buds with a mortar and pestle or grind them in an electric spice mill.

1 Put the milk in a heavy medium saucepan with the sugar and lavender. Warm over medium heat, stirring to dissolve the sugar, until small bubbles begin to appear around the edges of the pan. Remove from the heat, cover, and let steep at room temperature for 30 minutes.

2 Pour the lavender milk into a covered container and refrigerate until cold, 1 to 2 hours. Whisk in the lemon juice.

3 Pour into the canister of an ice cream maker and freeze according to the manufacturer's directions. Transfer the ice milk to a covered container and freeze until it is firm enough to scoop, at least 3 hours or overnight.

INGREDIENTS

4   cups whole or
    2 percent milk

1½ cups sugar

1   tablespoon dried lavender,
    finely crushed

1   tablespoon fresh
    lemon juice

Makes about 5 cups

COOL TIPS FOR SUCCESS

For best results purchase the culinary "Provence" lavender buds that are available at many gourmet shops and mail-order sources. It has a very low camphor level, a delicate floral note, and a subtle flavor. Other varieties can taste medicinal.

oneyed Light Ice Cream with Roasted Almonds

When using only three ingredients, it's especially important those items be of the highest quality. The honey in this recipe provides sweetness as well as body, so check your local farmers' market or apiary for a deep variety that's full of flavor.

1 In a large bowl, whisk together the half-and-half and honey until well blended. Cover and refrigerate until cold, about 1 hour.

2 Pour into the canister of an ice cream maker and freeze according to the manufacturer's directions. Add the almonds and process for 1 minute longer. Transfer the ice cream to a covered container and freeze until it is firm enough to scoop, at least 4 hours or overnight.

INGREDIENTS

4   cups half-and-half

1   cup honey, preferably wildflower, linden, or chestnut honey

¾   cup honey-roasted almonds, coarsely chopped

Makes about 5 cups

COOL TIPS FOR SUCCESS

Most ice cream makers are designed with a feed tube on the lid specifically for adding ingredients at the end. When the ice cream is done, pour your "add-ins" through the feed tube and process until incorporated, usually 30 to 60 seconds. To ensure chocolate or caramel keeps its integrity, freeze the bits briefly before adding.

Drambuie Ice Milk

Drambuie is a Scotch whisky-based liqueur sweetened with honey and flavored with herbs. The crème fraîche adds richness, as well as a pleasant tartness, so this is best served in single-scoop portions, with a small glass of Drambuie on the side or over the top.

1 In a heavy small saucepan, bring the Drambuie to a simmer over medium to medium-low heat. Cook until the liquid is reduced to about ¼ cup. (Watch carefully, adjusting the heat as needed; if the alcohol gets too hot, it can ignite.) Remove from the heat and transfer to a medium bowl. Stir in the sugar until dissolved. Let cool to room temperature.

2 Whisk in the milk. Cover and refrigerate until cold, at least 3 hours.

3 Whisk in the crème fraîche until well blended. Pour into the canister of an ice cream maker and freeze according to the manufacturer's directions. Transfer the ice milk to a covered container and freeze until it is firm enough to scoop, at least 3 hours or overnight.

INGREDIENTS

½ cup Drambuie liqueur

¾ cup sugar

1 cup cold milk

1 container (7½ ounces or 215 grams) crème fraîche

Makes about 3 cups

awberry Dream
Light Ice Cream

Choose the ripest fresh berries you can for this luscious no-cook ice cream, but trim off any bruised or damaged bits. If you use frozen, be sure to include any juices.

1 Working in batches if needed, puree the berries with half the sugar in a food processor or blender until smooth.

2 In a large bowl, whisk together the strawberry puree, half-and-half, orange juice concentrate, and remaining sugar. If you have time, cover and refrigerate for 1 to 2 hours to allow the flavors to develop.

3 Whisk the strawberry base to blend. Pour into the canister of an ice cream maker and freeze according to the manufacturer's directions. Transfer the ice cream to a covered container and freeze until it is firm enough to scoop, at least 4 hours or overnight.

INGREDIENTS

2   pints (900 ml) very ripe fresh strawberries, stemmed, or 2 packages (1 pound or 450 grams each) frozen unsweetened strawberries, partially thawed

1½ cups sugar

2   cups half-and-half

1   tablespoon frozen orange juice concentrate

Makes about 1 quart (1 liter)

Tangerine-Buttermilk Sherbet with Raspberry Swirl

Citrus makes a delicious complement to tangy buttermilk. Health food stores and many supermarkets now carry excellent fresh fruit juices in their refrigerated section. Faced with the prospect of juicing about 16 tangerines to get 2 cups of juice, you may opt for convenience. If plain tangerine juice is not available, try a blend like orange-tangerine.

1 In a food processor or blender, puree the raspberries with any juices until smooth. Strain through a medium sieve into a small nonreactive saucepan to remove the seeds. Press through as much of the fruit and juice as you can. Stir in ¼ cup of the sugar. Cook over medium-low heat, stirring often, until the raspberry puree thickens, about 10 minutes. Remove from the heat and let cool to room temperature; then cover and refrigerate until cold, at least 1 hour.

2 In a large bowl, combine the remaining 1¼ cups sugar with the buttermilk and tangerine juice. Stir until the sugar dissolves.

3 Pour the tangerine-buttermilk base into the canister of an ice cream maker and freeze according to the manufacturer's directions. Add the raspberry puree and process for 30 to 45 seconds, or just until swirled through. Transfer the sherbet to a covered container and freeze until it is firm enough to scoop, at least 4 hours or overnight.

INGREDIENTS

1   package (10 ounces or 275 grams) frozen unsweetened raspberries, thawed

1½ cups sugar

2   cups cold low-fat buttermilk

2   cups cold tangerine juice

Makes about 5 cups

COOL TIPS FOR SUCCESS

When creating a swirl with a sauce, add after the ice cream is done and churn for 30 to 60 seconds, until only partially blended. For a more defined swirl, do not add the sauce to the ice cream machine. Instead, working quickly, layer the finished ice cream and the sauce in a freezer container and run a blunt knife through the mixture several times, folding slightly, to create a marbleized effect.

Orange Sherbet

Don't expect the brilliant orange of some commercial brands of orange sherbet here. While the flavor is distinctive, the color is closest to cream. Any kind of orange juice can be used—fresh, frozen, reconstituted—but if it has pulp, strain before adding to achieve sherbet's characteristically smooth texture.

1 In a large bowl, combine the orange juice, sugar, and corn syrup. Stir to dissolve the sugar. Cover and refrigerate for 2 hours, or until very cold.

2 Whisk in the half-and-half and orange extract.

3 Pour into the canister of an ice cream maker and freeze according to the manufacturer's directions. Transfer the sherbet to a covered container and freeze until it is firm enough to scoop, at least 3 hours or overnight.

INGREDIENTS

2½ cups orange juice

⅓ cup sugar

1 tablespoon light corn syrup

1 cup half-and-half or whole milk

¼ teaspoon orange extract

Makes about 1 quart (1 liter)

Key Lime Sherbet

Of course, freshly squeezed fruit is best, but with bottled or frozen key lime juice available year round in the supermarket, it's nice to know you don't have to spend half an hour squeezing dozens of tiny key limes. To make an instant frozen key lime pie, pack the sherbet from the ice cream maker into a graham cracker crust, and return to the freezer. Just before serving, top the pie with sweetened whipped cream.

1 In a large bowl, combine the key lime juice and sugar. Stir to dissolve the sugar, then blend in the corn syrup and lime zest. Cover and refrigerate for 1 to 2 hours, or until very cold.

2 Whisk in the condensed milk. Pour into the canister of an ice cream maker and freeze according to the manufacturer's directions. Transfer the sherbet to a covered container and freeze until it is firm enough to scoop, at least 3 hours or overnight.

INGREDIENTS

1 cup key lime juice

¼ cup sugar

½ cup light corn syrup

1 tablespoon finely grated key lime zest, or use the zest from an ordinary lime

1 can (14 ounces or 400 grams) sweetened condensed milk

Makes about 3 cups

Banana Split Light Ice Cream

What could be better than all the flavors of a banana split locked up in a scoop of ice cream? This immensely satisfying flavor needs absolutely no garnish, though a single maraschino cherry on top would be a winsome touch.

1 Preheat the oven to 325°F (160°C). Spread out the pecans in a small baking dish and toast in the oven for 5 to 10 minutes, or until fragrant and very lightly browned. Transfer to a dish and let cool.

2 In a large bowl, combine the bananas, orange juice, sugar, and corn syrup. Mash with a fork to a coarse puree. Cover with plastic wrap pressed directly onto the surface so the bananas do not discolor. Refrigerate for 1 hour, or until cold.

3 Mix in the half-and-half and vanilla. Pour into the canister of an ice cream maker and freeze according to the manufacturer's directions. Add the pecans, chocolate chips, and cherries and process for 1 minute longer, or until incorporated. Transfer the ice cream to a covered container and freeze until it is firm enough to scoop, at least 3 hours or overnight.

INGREDIENTS

⅓ cup coarsely chopped pecans

2 very ripe medium bananas

1 tablespoon orange juice

½ cup sugar

2 tablespoons light corn syrup

2 cups half-and-half

2 teaspoons vanilla extract

⅓ cup semisweet chocolate chips

6 maraschino cherries, stemmed and chopped

Makes about 1½ pints (675 ml)

Boysenberry Buttermilk Sherbet

Boysenberries are an intense sweet dark berry, with a lot more flavor than blackberries. If you can't find them fresh, look for them frozen. Blackberries or raspberries can be substituted. As in baking, buttermilk, rather than ordinary milk or cream, adds a wonderful hint of tang with very little fat.

1 If using fresh berries, rinse gently and drain in a colander. Pick over to remove any badly bruised or moldy fruit.

2 In a food processor or blender, combine the boysenberries, ¾ cup sugar, and the lemon juice. Puree until smooth.

3 Strain the berry mixture into a large bowl to remove the seeds, pressing through as much of the juice and fruit as you can. Stir in the corn syrup. Taste and add more sugar, 1 tablespoon at a time, if you think it's needed. Cover and refrigerate for 2 hours, or until very cold.

4 Whisk in the buttermilk. Pour into the canister of an ice cream maker and freeze according to the manufacturer's directions. Transfer the sherbet to a covered container and freeze until it is firm enough to scoop, at least 3 hours or overnight.

INGREDIENTS

3 cups fresh boysenberries (1½ pints or 675 ml) or frozen unsweetened boysenberries, partially thawed

¾ to 1 cup sugar

1 teaspoon fresh lemon juice

1 tablespoon light corn syrup

2 cups cold buttermilk

Makes about 1 quart (1 liter)

Ginger Bite Light Ice Cream

Pungent ground dried ginger and mellower crystallized ginger add up to a grown-up ice cream with a bit of a bite. Dress up, if you like, with a drizzle of Bittersweet Fudge Sauce (page 184) and pass a plate of buttery Scottish shortbread or sugar cookies on the side.

1 In a large bowl, whisk together the half-and-half, sugar, ground ginger, and vanilla. If you have time, cover the mixture and refrigerate for an hour to allow the flavors to develop.

2 Pour the mixture into the canister of an ice cream maker and freeze according to the manufacturer's directions. Add the crystallized ginger and process for 1 minute longer. Transfer the ice cream to a covered container and freeze until it is firm enough to scoop, at least 3 hours or overnight.

INGREDIENTS

4   cups half-and-half
1½ cups sugar
2   teaspoons ground ginger
1   teaspoon vanilla extract
¾   cup chopped crystallized
     ginger

Makes about 5 cups

COOL TIPS FOR SUCCESS

Many sorbets and ice creams that are non-custard based become hard in the freezer. Let them stand at room temperature for 5 minutes until softened enough to scoop.

Peppermint Candy Light Ice Cream

Ordinary red and white round peppermint candies combine with peppermint extract for a bracing frozen dessert especially for mint lovers. For the full treatment, serve with Peppermint Fudge Sauce (page 117).

1 In a heavy medium saucepan, bring the milk to a simmer over medium heat. Cook, stirring, for about 3 minutes, or until the mixture is hot and bubbles just begin to form at the edges. Remove from the heat.

2 Beat the egg yolks lightly in a medium bowl. Gradually whisk in about 1 cup of the warm milk. Return the egg mixture to the saucepan, reduce the heat to medium-low, and cook, stirring, until the custard thickens enough to coat the back of a spoon, 170° to 175°F (75° to 80°C). Do not boil, or the egg yolks will curdle.

3 Strain the custard into a large bowl. Whisk in the sweetened condensed milk. Refrigerate, covered, until the custard is very cold, at least 4 hours.

4 Stir in half of the crushed peppermint candies, the vanilla, and the peppermint extract. Pour the custard into the canister of an ice cream maker and freeze according to the manufacturer's directions.

5 Add the remaining crushed peppermint candies and process for 1 minute longer, or until incorporated. Transfer the ice cream to a covered container and freeze until it is firm enough to scoop, at least 4 hours or overnight.

INGREDIENTS

2½ cups whole milk

2 egg yolks

1 can (14 ounces or 400 grams) sweetened condensed milk

⅔ cup crushed peppermint candies (about 5 ounces or 150 grams)

1 teaspoon vanilla extract

½ teaspoon peppermint extract

Makes about 1 quart (1 liter)

Frozen Hot Chocolate

Yes, this frosty dessert does taste as good as it sounds. Hold on to that image of a deep, dark chocolaty drink and then imagine it instantly frozen, melting on the tongue. That's what this iced treat is all about.

1 In a heavy large saucepan, combine the half-and-half, sugar, and salt. Bring to a simmer over medium heat, stirring, for about 5 minutes, or until the sugar dissolves and the mixture is hot. Remove from the heat and whisk in the cocoa powder until well blended. Add the chopped chocolate and stir until melted and smooth. Let stand for 15 minutes to cool slightly, then whisk in the vanilla. Cover and refrigerate for 2 hours, or until very cold.

2 Stir the chocolate base to blend and pour into the canister of an ice cream maker. Freeze according to the manufacturer's directions. Eat at once while soft and somewhat slushy, or transfer to a covered container and freeze for up to 4 hours.

3 Serve in large goblets or mugs, with a spoon and a straw. Top with marshmallows or whipped cream, and a dusting of shaved chocolate or a few chocolate curls.

INGREDIENTS

3   cups half-and-half

¾   cup sugar

Dash of salt

½   cup Dutch process unsweetened cocoa powder

2   ounces (50 grams) bittersweet or semisweet chocolate, finely chopped

1   teaspoon vanilla extract

Marshmallows or whipped cream, for garnish

Shaved chocolate or Chocolate Curls (page 187), for garnish

Makes about 1 quart (1 liter)

Dark Chocolate Ice Milk

In between an ice cream and a sorbet, this light chocolate frozen dessert is both refreshing and satisfying. Adorn, if you like, with a drizzle of chocolate or raspberry sauce.

1 In a heavy medium saucepan, whisk the cocoa powder into the water until smooth. Whisk in the sugar, milk, and salt. Bring to a boil over medium heat, stirring constantly, until the sugar is dissolved. Remove from the heat. Whisk in the corn syrup.

2 Cover and refrigerate for at least 4 hours, or until very cold. Whisk in the vanilla to blend.

3 Pour into the canister of an ice cream maker and freeze according to the manufacturer's directions. Transfer the ice milk to a covered container and freeze until it is firm enough to scoop, at least 3 hours or overnight.

INGREDIENTS

⅔ cup Dutch process unsweetened cocoa powder

1½ cups water

1 cup sugar

1 cup whole milk

Dash of salt

1 tablespoon light corn syrup

½ teaspoon vanilla extract

Makes about 1 quart (1 liter)

Peanut Butter
Light Ice Cream

Creamy peanut butter adds body, texture, and richness to this egg-free ice cream. It's luscious served *au natural*, and even better drizzled with your favorite chocolate sauce and showered with chopped roasted peanuts.

1 In a large bowl, combine the half-and-half, sugar, and salt. Whisk until well blended. Gradually whisk in the peanut butter and vanilla. If you have time, cover and refrigerate for 1 to 2 hours to allow the flavors to develop.

2 Pour into the canister of an ice cream maker and freeze according to the manufacturer's directions. Transfer to a covered container and freeze for 1 to 4 hours before serving.

INGREDIENTS

3   cups half-and-half
⅔   cup sugar
Dash of salt
¾   cup smooth peanut butter
1   teaspoon vanilla extract

Makes about 1 quart (1 liter)

COOL TIPS FOR SUCCESS

Do not use an "old-fashioned" or "natural" peanut butter, which separates and becomes oily.

"enjoy your ice cream while
it's on your plate–
that's my philosophy."

–playwright Thornton Wilder

frozen yogurts
& soy ice milks

Jamaican Banana
Frozen Yogurt

Bananas, lime, and coconut conjure up a great cold dessert for a warm summer night. To be sure the flavor is as intense as it should be, plan ahead so your bananas are overripe; the skins should be heavily speckled with brown spots.

1 Combine the sugar and water in a small saucepan. Cook over medium heat, stirring until the sugar dissolves. Boil the syrup without stirring for 2 minutes. Pour into a large heatproof bowl and let cool.

2 Add the bananas and mash with a fork until no large chunks remain. Stir in the yogurt, lime juice, and coconut extract. Cover and refrigerate for 2 hours, or until cold.

3 Pour the yogurt base into the canister of an ice cream maker and freeze according to the manufacturer's directions. Transfer the frozen yogurt to a covered container and freeze until it is firm enough to scoop, at least 4 hours or overnight.

INGREDIENTS

1   cup sugar
1   cup water
2   overripe medium bananas
2   cups plain yogurt
1½ teaspoons fresh lime juice
1   teaspoon coconut extract

Makes about 1 quart (1 liter)

Golden Vanilla-Apricot Frozen Yogurt

Lyle's Golden Syrup, imported from England, contributes a caramelized quality that simply can't be matched. The sweetener can be found in tins alongside the corn syrup in many well-stocked supermarkets and in stores that specialize in imported foods. If it is not available in your area, substitute a good, flavorful honey.

1 Place the chopped apricots in a bowl and add enough hot water to cover. Let stand for about 15 minutes to soften. Drain well. Cover and refrigerate until needed.

2 In a medium bowl, whisk together the yogurt, syrup, and vanilla until well blended. If you have time, cover and refrigerate the yogurt base for 1 to 2 hours to allow the flavors to develop.

3 Pour the yogurt base into the canister of an ice cream maker and freeze according to the manufacturer's directions. Add the chopped apricots and process for 1 minute longer, or until incorporated. Serve at once while still soft, or transfer to a covered container and freeze for 1 to 4 hours before serving.

INGREDIENTS

½ cup finely chopped dried apricots

3 cups plain yogurt

1 cup Lyle's Golden Syrup or honey

2 teaspoons vanilla extract

Makes about 1 quart (1 liter)

Toasted Almond and Apricot Frozen Yogurt

Apricots and almonds are a perfect pairing. Here they transform low-fat yogurt into a stellar dessert that's lean and luscious at the same time.

1 Preheat the oven to 325°F (160°C). Spread out the almonds on a baking sheet and toast in the oven for 8 to 10 minutes, stirring once or twice, until lightly browned and fragrant. Transfer the nuts to a dish and let cool.

2 Drain the apricots, reserving ¼ cup of the syrup. Chop 3 apricot halves into bite-size pieces; refrigerate until needed. In a food processor, puree the remaining apricots until smooth. Scrape into a large bowl.

3 Add the reserved apricot syrup, the yogurt, brown sugar, lemon juice, almond extract, and salt to the pureed apricots. Mix until well blended. Cover and refrigerate for 2 hours, or until very cold.

4 Pour the yogurt base into the canister of an ice cream maker and freeze according to the manufacturer's directions. Add the reserved apricots and toasted almonds and process for 1 minute longer or until incorporated. Transfer the frozen yogurt to a covered container and freeze until it is firm enough to scoop, at least 4 hours or overnight.

INGREDIENTS

½   cup slivered almonds, coarsely chopped

1   can (16 ounces or 450 grams) apricot halves in heavy syrup

2   cups low-fat custard-style vanilla yogurt

½   cup (packed) light brown sugar

1   teaspoon fresh lemon juice

½   teaspoon almond extract

Dash of salt

Makes about 1 quart (1 liter)

Lemon Drop Frozen Yogurt

Here's a delightful lemon frozen dessert that can be thrown together in minutes. It's good on its own, sublime with a drizzle of Raspberry Sauce.

1 In a medium bowl, combine the yogurt, sugar, and lemon zest. Stir to dissolve the sugar. If you have time, cover and refrigerate for 1 to 2 hours to allow the flavors to develop.

2 Pour the yogurt into the canister of an ice cream maker and freeze according to the manufacturer's directions. Serve at once while still soft or transfer to a covered container and freeze for 1 to 4 hours before serving.

Raspberry Sauce

1 If using fresh berries, rinse gently and drain in a colander. Pick over to remove any bruised or moldy fruit.

2 In a food processor or blender, puree the raspberries until smooth. Strain through a medium sieve into a bowl to remove the seeds. Press through as much of the fruit and juices as you can. Stir in the sugar and lemon juice. Let stand for 2 or 3 minutes, or until the sugar dissolves. Taste and stir in more sugar if needed. Serve at once or cover and refrigerate for up to 3 days. Freeze for longer storage. Serve chilled or at room temperature.

INGREDIENTS

3 cups lemon-flavored whole milk yogurt

⅔ to ¾ cup sugar, to taste

Finely grated zest of 2 lemons

Makes about 1 quart (1 liter)

Raspberry Sauce

1½ cups fresh or thawed frozen unsweetened raspberries

3 tablespoons sugar

1 teaspoon fresh lemon juice

Makes about ¾ cup

VARIATION

Lemon-Ginger Frozen Yogurt: When the yogurt reaches the soft-serve stage, add about ⅔ cup of finely chopped crystallized ginger and process for 1 minute longer or until incorporated.

Pink Lemonade Soy Sherbet

Dairy free, this delightful sweet-tart sherbet gets its touch of creaminess from silken tofu. Best of all, no one will know it's there unless you tell them.

1 In a food processor or blender, combine the pink lemonade concentrate, tofu, and corn syrup. Process until smooth. Add the water and pulse several times until well blended. Scrape the mixture into a large bowl. Cover and refrigerate for 2 hours, or until very cold.

2 Stir to blend and pour into the canister of an ice cream maker. Freeze according to the manufacturer's directions. Eat at once or transfer to a covered container and freeze for 1 to 4 hours before serving.

INGREDIENTS

1 large can (12 ounces or 350 grams) frozen pink lemonade concentrate

12 ounces (350 grams) silken tofu

¼ cup light corn syrup

1½ cups water

Makes about 5 cups

COOL TIPS FOR SUCCESS

To prevent ice crystals from forming when ice cream is taken in and out of the freezer, cover any open container with plastic wrap pressed directly onto the surface of the ice cream before closing the lid.

Spiced Plum Frozen Yogurt

Santa Rosa plums, those firm black plums uniformly sweet and not too tart, are the first choice here, though other varieties could be substituted. Plums contain plenty of pectin, the natural thickener that helps jams to set, so this iced yogurt has a good deal of body.

1 Put the plums in a nonreactive medium saucepan and add the sugar, cardamom, cinnamon, and cloves. Cook over medium heat, stirring often, until the plums are very soft, about 10 minutes. Strain through a medium sieve into a large bowl, pressing through as much of the fruit as you can. Discard the plum skins and any stringy fibers. Stir in the lemon juice. Cover and refrigerate for 2 hours, or until cold.

2 Whisk the yogurt into the chilled spiced plum puree.

3 Pour into the canister of an ice cream maker and freeze according to the manufacturer's directions. Transfer the frozen yogurt to a covered container and freeze until it is firm enough to scoop, at least 4 hours or overnight.

INGREDIENTS

1½ cups coarsely chopped pitted Santa Rosa plums (about 6 to 8 plums)

⅔ cup sugar

1 teaspoon ground cardamom

½ teaspoon ground cinnamon

Dash of cloves

2 tablespoons fresh lemon juice

3 cups vanilla-flavored whole milk yogurt, chilled

Makes about 1 quart (1 liter)

Brown Sugar–Pineapple Iced Soy Milk

Here's proof a heart-healthy dessert can be as hedonistic as the next. Soy delivers a remarkably rich ice milk, especially tempting when paired with caramel-like brown sugar and chewy bits of candied pineapple.

1 In a large bowl, whisk together the soy milk and brown sugar until the sugar dissolves. Whisk in the vanilla to blend. If you have time, cover and refrigerate for 1 to 2 hours to allow the flavors to develop.

2 Pour into the canister of an ice cream maker and freeze according to the manufacturer's directions. Add the candied pineapple and process for 1 minute longer. Transfer the iced soy milk to a covered container and freeze until firm enough to scoop, at least 3 hours or overnight.

INGREDIENTS

4   cups cold plain soy milk
1   cup (packed) dark brown sugar
1½ teaspoons vanilla extract
1   cup coarsely chopped candied pineapple rings

Makes about 5 cups

Rhubarb-Raspberry Frozen Yogurt

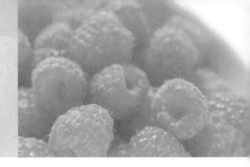

An old cook's maxim advises pairing fruits that come into season at the same time, so the combination of these two makes perfect sense. The result is a wonderful frozen dessert that is delightfully tart, sweet, and intense.

1 In a nonreactive medium saucepan, combine the rhubarb, sugar, and water. Cook over medium heat for about 7 minutes, stirring frequently, until the rhubarb is soft. Set aside for 10 minutes to cool slightly.

2 In a food processor, puree the rhubarb until smooth. Scrape into a large bowl and stir in the yogurt, raspberries, corn syrup, and orange extract. Cover and refrigerate for 2 hours, or until cold.

3 Pour the yogurt into the canister of an ice cream maker and freeze according to the manufacturer's directions. Transfer the frozen yogurt to a covered container and freeze until it is firm enough to scoop, at least 4 hours or overnight.

INGREDIENTS

4 cups sliced fresh rhubarb or thawed frozen rhubarb (about 1 pound or 450 grams)

¾ cup sugar

½ cup water

2 cups plain yogurt

1 cup fresh or thawed frozen raspberries

1 tablespoon light corn syrup

½ teaspoon orange extract

Makes about 5 cups

Black Forest Frozen Yogurt with Chocolate and Cherries

Just like with the cake, Black Forest here indicates cherries and chocolate. The combination creates a smashing flavor that makes a hedonistic frozen yogurt.

1 If using fresh cherries, remove any stems. Rinse well and pat dry with paper towels. Working over a bowl to catch the juices, cut the cherries in half with a small, sharp stainless steel knife. Cut out the pit with the tip of the knife and drop the cherries into the bowl.

2 Add the sugar to the cherries and toss to mix well. Stir in the yogurt, lemon juice, and almond extract. Stir to dissolve the sugar. If you have time, cover and refrigerate for 1 to 2 hours to allow the flavors to develop.

3 Pour the yogurt base into the canister of an ice cream maker and freeze according to the manufacturer's directions. Add the chocolate and process for 1 minute longer, or until incorporated. Transfer the frozen yogurt to a covered container and freeze until it is firm enough to scoop, at least 4 hours or overnight.

INGREDIENTS

¾ pound (12 ounces or 350 grams) fresh sweet cherries or 1½ cups frozen unsweetened Bing cherries, thawed

⅔ cup sugar

3 cups vanilla-flavored yogurt

1 tablespoon fresh lemon juice

¼ teaspoon almond extract

3 ounces (75 grams) bittersweet or semisweet chocolate chunks, coarsely chopped and chilled

Makes about 5 cups

Chocolate Frozen Yogurt with Walnuts and Marshmallows

In frozen desserts, this mix of chocolate and extras has long been dubbed "rocky road." No matter the name, it's a voluptuous combo that appeals to both young and old alike.

1 Preheat the oven to 325°F (160°C). Spread out the walnuts in a small baking pan and toast in the oven until fragrant and very lightly browned, 7 to 10 minutes. Transfer to a plate and let cool, then coarsely chop.

2 In a medium bowl, combine the yogurt, sugar, cocoa powder, vanilla, and salt. Stir to dissolve the sugar. If you have time, cover and refrigerate for 1 to 2 hours to allow the flavors to develop.

3 Pour the yogurt base into the canister of an ice cream maker and freeze according to the manufacturer's directions. Add the chopped toasted walnuts and the marshmallows and process for 1 minute longer, or until incorporated. Transfer the frozen yogurt to a covered container and freeze until it is firm enough to scoop, at least 3 hours or overnight.

INGREDIENTS

¾ cup walnut pieces

4 cups plain yogurt

1 cup sugar

½ cup Dutch process unsweetened cocoa powder

1½ teaspoons vanilla extract

Dash of salt

¾ cup miniature marshmallows

Makes about 1½ quarts (1½ liters)

COOL TIPS FOR SUCCESS

Finished ice cream benefits from a few hours in the freezer to "ripen." During this time the ice cream becomes firm enough to scoop, and the flavors develop further.

Mocha–Chocolate Chip Iced Soy Milk

Dairy-free and delightful, this chocolate- and coffee-flavored frozen yogurt laced with chocolate chips could fool anyone into thinking it's a decadent dessert. For proper texture, be sure the tofu you purchase is "silken," the softest kind.

1 In a heavy medium saucepan, combine the chocolate soy milk, sugar, espresso powder, and salt. Bring to a simmer over medium heat, stirring, until the sugar dissolves and the liquid is hot, about 5 minutes. Remove from the heat and whisk in the cocoa powder until well blended. Add the chopped chocolate and stir until melted and smooth.

2 In a food processor or blender, puree the tofu until smooth. With the machine running, slowly pour in the warm chocolate mixture. Transfer to a bowl, cover, and refrigerate until cold, at least 4 hours. Whisk in the vanilla.

3 Pour the mocha base into the canister of an ice cream maker and freeze according to the manufacturer's directions. Add the chocolate chips and process for 30 seconds to 1 minute longer, or until incorporated. Transfer the iced soy milk to a covered container and freeze until firm enough to scoop, at least 3 hours or overnight.

INGREDIENTS

1½ cups chocolate soy milk

1 cup sugar

1½ teaspoons instant espresso powder

Dash of salt

2 tablespoons unsweetened cocoa powder

2 ounces (50 grams) bittersweet or semisweet chocolate, finely chopped

1 pound (450 grams) silken tofu

1 teaspoon vanilla extract

¾ cup chocolate chips, chilled

Makes about 1 quart (1 liter)

Double Chocolate Frozen Yogurt

As lovers of some of the better brands of frozen yogurt know, you can feel virtuous and still have a rollicking good time with flavors like this one. Dutch process cocoa is important here for deep flavor and color.

1 In a medium bowl, combine the yogurt, sugar, cocoa powder, vanilla, and salt. Stir to dissolve the sugar. If you have time, cover and refrigerate for 1 to 2 hours to allow the flavors to develop.

2 Pour the yogurt base into the canister of an ice cream maker and freeze according to the manufacturer's directions. Add the semisweet chocolate chips and process for 1 minute longer, or until incorporated. Transfer the frozen yogurt to a covered container and freeze until it is firm enough to scoop, at least 4 hours or overnight.

INGREDIENTS

3   cups plain yogurt

¾   cup sugar

6   tablespoons Dutch process unsweetened cocoa powder

1   teaspoon vanilla extract

Dash of salt

¾   cup semisweet chocolate chips or chopped bittersweet chocolate, chilled

Makes about 1 quart (1 liter)

Quick Cinnamon–Candy Crunch Frozen Yogurt

Everyone needs a few "quick fix" recipes for those days when time is short and demands are high. Vietnamese or other best-quality ground cinnamon magically transforms store-bought vanilla frozen yogurt into an exotic flavor all your own. For added decadence, chopped candy does the trick. How quick is that?

1 Let the frozen yogurt soften slightly at room temperature for 10 to 15 minutes—it should be malleable but not liquid. Use a heavy rubber spatula or large wooden spoon to mix in the cinnamon until well blended. Working quickly, fold in the candy.

2 Scrape the frozen yogurt back into the carton and cover with plastic wrap, pressing against the surface to prevent air pockets. Freeze until firm, at least 6 hours or up to 2 weeks.

INGREDIENTS

1 quart (1 liter) vanilla frozen yogurt

2 tablespoons ground cinnamon

1 cup coarsely chopped chocolate- and nut-covered toffee candy, such as Almond Roca® buttercrunch, chilled

Makes about 1 quart (1 liter)

COOL TIPS FOR SUCCESS

Store ice cream in the coldest part of the freezer—not in the door. If the original packaging of store-bought ice cream does not appear airtight, enclose the container in a large freezer-safe zippered plastic bag.

"you never really know your friends
from your enemies
until the ice breaks."

–old Eskimo proverb

sorbets,
granitas,
& ices

Apricot Sorbet

Because apricot season is so painfully brief, and ripe fresh apricots are hard to come by in many regions, this recipe makes it easy by preparing the sorbet with canned. And because the fruit has already been packed in heavy syrup, there's no need to make a simple syrup and let it cool first, which makes this a quick and easy dessert.

1 Drain the apricots, reserving ½ cup of the syrup.

2 In a food processor or blender, puree the apricots until smooth. Transfer to a large bowl. Whisk in the reserved ½ cup syrup, the sugar, lemon juice, corn syrup, and apricot brandy. Cover and refrigerate for 2 hours, or until the sugar is dissolved and the mixture is very cold.

3 Whisk to blend and pour into the canister of an ice cream maker. Freeze according to the manufacturer's directions. Transfer the sorbet to a covered container and freeze until it is firm enough to scoop, at least 3 hours or overnight.

INGREDIENTS

2 cans (16 ounces or 450 grams each) apricot halves in heavy syrup

¾ cup sugar

1 tablespoon fresh lemon juice

1 tablespoon light corn syrup

1 tablespoon apricot brandy, plain brandy, or amaretto

Makes about 3 cups

Almost-Instant Apple Ice

Quick and convenient, here's an ice that's poured immediately into the ice cream maker. Enjoy as a slush when it comes out of the machine, or as an ice as soon as it firms up in the freezer.

1 In a large bowl, combine the cold apple juice, the apple juice concentrate, lemon juice, Calvados, and corn syrup. Whisk to blend.

2 Pour into the canister of an ice cream maker and freeze according to the manufacturer's directions. Eat at once, while still somewhat slushy, or transfer to a covered container and freeze for at least 2 hours, until firm.

INGREDIENTS

3 cups unsweetened apple juice or fresh cider, well chilled

1 can (6 ounces or 175 grams) frozen unsweetened apple juice concentrate, thawed but still very cold

2 tablespoons fresh lemon juice

1 tablespoon Calvados, applejack, or brandy

1 tablespoon light corn syrup

Makes about 1 quart (1 liter)

Green Apple Sorbet

Subtle yet distinctive and traditional in France, this mildly tart sorbet is an excellent dessert to serve after a substantial meal. Garnish with a few very thin slices of unpeeled green apples and douse each dish, if you like, with an extra splash of Calvados.

1 In a small saucepan, combine the apple juice, sugar, and cinnamon stick. Cook over medium heat, stirring often, until the sugar dissolves. Boil the syrup without stirring for 2 minutes. Remove from the heat, cover, and let stand at room temperature for 1 hour so that the syrup cools slowly and absorbs the cinnamon flavor.

2 Peel and core the apples and cut them into eighths. Place in a medium saucepan with the lemon juice, salt, and just enough water to cover. Cook over medium heat until the apples are soft, about 10 minutes; drain. Transfer the cooked apples to a food processor and puree until the applesauce is smooth.

3 Discard the cinnamon stick from the syrup. Whisk the cinnamon syrup and the Calvados into the applesauce. Transfer to a covered container and refrigerate for 2 hours, or until very cold.

4 Whisk to blend and pour into the canister of an ice cream maker. Freeze according to the manufacturer's directions. Transfer the sorbet to a covered container and freeze until firm enough to scoop, at least 3 hours or overnight.

INGREDIENTS

1½ cups unsweetened apple juice

½ cup sugar

1 cinnamon stick

3 large tart green apples, such as Granny Smith (about 1½ pounds or 675 grams)

3 tablespoons fresh lemon juice

Dash of salt

2 tablespoons Calvados, applejack, apple brandy, or green apple liqueur

Makes about 1 quart (1 liter)

Meyer Lemon Sorbet

Meyer lemons are usually available from November through May. They're less tart than the ordinary varieties and taste a bit of mandarin orange. During other times of the year, or if Meyer lemons are not in your market, just use any common lemon and substitute fresh orange juice for about 2 tablespoons of the lemon juice to mellow the acidity.

1 Combine the sugar and water in a small saucepan. Cook over medium heat, stirring often, until the sugar dissolves. Boil the syrup without stirring for 2 minutes. Remove from the heat and let cool to room temperature.

2 Stir in the lemon juice, lemon zest, corn syrup, and vodka. Cover and refrigerate for 1 to 2 hours, or until very cold.

3 Pour into the canister of an ice cream maker. Freeze according to the manufacturer's directions. Transfer the sorbet to a covered container and freeze until it is firm enough to scoop, at least 3 hours or overnight.

INGREDIENTS

1   cup sugar

1   cup water

1   cup Meyer lemon juice
    (from 6 to 8 lemons)

2   teaspoons finely grated
    Meyer lemon zest

2   tablespoons light corn
    syrup

1   tablespoon lemon-flavored
    vodka, limoncello,
    or plain vodka

Makes about 3 cups

Grapefruit Sorbet with Campari and Mint

Campari is an Italian liqueur that contributes both flavor and color to this sophisticated ice. Balance is key here, so do not be tempted to add any additional liqueur, or the sorbet may turn bitter.

1 In a large bowl, combine the grapefruit juice, sugar, Campari, corn syrup, and grenadine. Whisk to blend. Cover and refrigerate for 2 hours, or until very cold.

2 Pour into the canister of an ice cream maker and freeze according to the manufacturer's directions. Transfer the sorbet to a covered container and freeze until it is firm enough to scoop, at least 3 hours or overnight.

3 To serve, scoop the sorbet into chilled stemmed glasses or bowls. Drizzle about 1½ tablespoons Campari-Mint Syrup over each serving and garnish with a mint sprig. Serve at once.

Campari-Mint Syrup

1 In a small saucepan, combine the sugar, water, and mint sprig. Bring to a boil over medium heat, stirring to dissolve the sugar. Reduce the heat to medium-low and simmer for 10 minutes without stirring. Cover and remove from the heat. Let cool to room temperature.

2 Strain the mint syrup into a bowl. Discard the mint sprig. Stir 3 tablespoons of the Campari into the syrup. Taste and add more Campari if needed. Cover and refrigerate for 2 hours, or until very cold. Just before serving, stir in the shredded mint.

INGREDIENTS

2   cups pink or Ruby Red grapefruit juice, preferably fresh

1   cup sugar

1   tablespoon Campari or vodka

1   tablespoon light corn syrup

1   to 2 teaspoons grenadine, to taste

⅔   cup Campari-Mint Syrup (recipe follows)

Fresh mint sprigs, for garnish

Makes about 3 cups

Campari-Mint Syrup

½   cup sugar

½   cup water

1   large sprig of mint, plus 1 tablespoon shredded fresh mint leaves

3 to 4 tablespoons Campari

Makes about ⅔ cup

Honey-Melon Granita

Even though melon is a mild fruit, when it's perfectly ripe and full of flavor, it makes a delicious frozen dessert. Because the melon contains so much water, no syrup is needed. Honey acts as a sweetener and contributes body to the ice.

INGREDIENTS

6   cups diced very ripe cantaloupe or other sweet, fragrant melon

¾   cup honey

3   tablespoons fresh lemon or lime juice

Dash of salt

Makes about 1 quart (1 liter)

1 Working in batches if necessary, puree the melon in a food processor until smooth. With the machine running, add the honey, lemon juice, and salt. Transfer the melon puree to a bowl, cover, and refrigerate for 2 hours, or until very cold.

2 Pour into a shallow 8- or 9-inch (20- or 23-cm) square metal baking pan and cover with plastic wrap. Freeze for 45 minutes, or until the granita is frozen around the edges and the surface is covered with a thin layer of ice. Using a fork, break up the ice, scraping the crystals from the edges of the pan and mixing them into the center to distribute evenly.

3 Return the pan, covered, to the freezer for about 30 minutes, or until the edges have frozen again. Repeat the process at least 3 more times, scraping, mixing, and re-freezing until large, granular ice crystals have formed and the mixture is light and slightly slushy. Do not let the granita harden into a solid mass. Serve at once, or cover and freeze for up to 4 hours.

VARIATION

Honey-Melon Ice: Refrigerate the honey-melon puree until cold. Whisk to blend and pour into the canister of an ice cream maker. Freeze according to the manufacturer's directions, until the mixture is frozen and spoonable but not hard or crumbly. Serve at once, or transfer to a covered container and freeze for at least 30 minutes before serving.

Pear Sorbet with Cabernet Syrup and Fresh Basil

Canned pears make a remarkably fresh-tasting instant sorbet—with no peeling and no poaching.

1 In a food processor or blender, puree the pears until smooth. Transfer to a large bowl.

2 Whisk in 1 cup of the Cabernet Syrup, the lemon juice, and corn syrup. Cover and refrigerate for 2 hours, or until very cold.

3 Stir in the chopped basil and pour into the canister of an ice cream maker. Freeze according to the manufacturer's directions. Transfer the sorbet to a covered container and freeze until it is firm enough to scoop, at least 3 hours or overnight.

4 To serve, scoop the sorbet into chilled stemmed glasses or bowls. Drizzle 1 or 2 tablespoons of the remaining Cabernet Syrup over each serving and garnish with a small sprig of basil. Serve at once.

Cabernet Syrup

1 In a nonreactive small saucepan, combine the wine, sugar, basil leaves, and lemon zest. Bring to a boil over medium heat, stirring to dissolve the sugar. Reduce the heat to medium-low and simmer for 10 minutes without stirring. Cover and remove from the heat. Let cool to room temperature.

2 Strain the wine syrup to remove the basil and lemon. Refrigerate, covered, for 2 hours, or until cold.

INGREDIENTS

1 can (16 ounces or 450 grams) sliced Bartlett pears in heavy syrup, drained

1½ cups Cabernet Syrup (recipe follows)

1 tablespoon fresh lemon juice

1 tablespoon light corn syrup

5 fresh basil leaves, finely chopped

Small sprigs of basil, for garnish

Makes about 1 quart (1 liter)

Cabernet Syrup

1½ cups Cabernet Sauvignon, or other dry red wine

¾ cup sugar

4 large fresh basil leaves

1 strip of lemon zest (2 by 1½ inches, or 5 by 3¾ cm)

Makes about 1½ cups

Mango-Pineapple Sorbet

Fresh tropical fruits naturally impart plenty of body to this lush sorbet, so there is no need to make a sugar syrup first. The sugar dissolves during the initial chilling time in the refrigerator. Ripe pineapples are not only easy to find these days, you can buy a whole fruit or just the amount you need already cut into chunks in the produce or refrigerated section of your supermarket.

1 Peel the mangoes and cut the fruit away from the large flat pit. In a food processor or blender, puree the mango until smooth. There should be about 3 cups of puree.

2 Transfer to a large bowl. Stir in the chopped pineapple, sugar, lime juice, and rum. Cover and refrigerate until very cold, at least 2 hours or as long as 2 days.

3 Stir the mixture to blend and pour into the canister of an ice cream maker. Freeze according to the manufacturer's directions. Transfer the sorbet to a covered container and freeze until it is firm enough to scoop, at least 3 hours or overnight.

INGREDIENTS

3 ripe large mangoes (about 2¼ pounds or 1 kg total)

1 cup finely chopped fresh pineapple (about 6 ounces or 175 grams)

⅔ cup sugar

3 tablespoons fresh lime juice

1 tablespoon light rum or vodka

Makes about 1 quart (1 liter)

Mojito Sorbet

Here's the hottest drink on the bar circuit transformed into a spoonable dessert. Garnish with sprigs of fresh mint or thin slices of lime bent into a twist.

1 In a small saucepan, combine the sugar, water, and mint sprigs. Cook over medium heat, stirring often, until the sugar dissolves. Boil the syrup without stirring for 2 minutes. Remove from the heat, cover, and let steep at room temperature for 30 minutes.

2 Strain the mint syrup into a bowl and discard the mint sprigs. Stir in the lime juice, lime zest, rum, and corn syrup. Cover and refrigerate for 2 hours, or until very cold.

3 Pour the mojito base into the canister of an ice cream maker. Freeze according to the manufacturer's directions. Add the slivered mint leaves and process for 1 minute longer. Transfer the sorbet to a covered container and freeze until it is firm enough to scoop, at least 3 hours or overnight.

INGREDIENTS

1	cup sugar
2	cups water
5	large sprigs of fresh mint plus 1½ tablespoons slivered mint leaves
1	cup fresh lime juice
1	teaspoon finely grated lime zest
2	tablespoons light rum
1	tablespoon light corn syrup

Makes about 3 cups

Gin & Tonic Ice with Lime

Because of the amount of alcohol in this adult dessert, it never freezes as solid as an ordinary ice. Think of it as a frozen cocktail and serve with both a spoon and a straw.

1 In a large bowl, combine the sugar, gin, lime juice, and lime zest. Stir to blend and dissolve the sugar. Cover and refrigerate for 30 minutes, or until very cold.

2 Gradually stir in the tonic water. Pour into the canister of an ice cream maker and freeze according to the manufacturer's directions.

3 Scrape the slush into tall, chilled glasses and garnish the edge of each glass with a slice of lime. Serve at once, with a long-handled iced tea spoon and a long straw.

INGREDIENTS

¾   cup sugar

⅓   cup gin

¼   cup fresh lime juice

1   tablespoon finely grated lime zest

1   bottle (28 ounces or 800 grams) tonic water, chilled

Lime slices, for garnish

Makes about 5 cups

Spiced Cranberry Sorbet

Fresh cranberries are a highly seasonal fruit, but this sweetly spiced sorbet is conveniently made with bottled cranberry juice. Decorate each serving with a cinnamon stick, if you like.

1 In a small saucepan, combine the sugar, water, cinnamon stick, and cloves. Cook over medium heat, stirring often, until the sugar dissolves. Boil the syrup without stirring for 1 minute. Reduce the heat to low and simmer for 2 minutes longer. Remove the pan from the heat and let sit, covered, for 30 minutes at room temperature.

2 Strain the syrup into a large heatproof bowl and discard the cinnamon stick and cloves. Stir in the cranberry juice, vodka, and corn syrup. Cover and refrigerate for 2 hours, or until very cold.

3 Whisk to blend and pour into the canister of an ice cream maker. Freeze according to the manufacturer's directions. Transfer to a covered container and freeze until firm enough to scoop, at least 3 hours or overnight.

INGREDIENTS

1½ cups sugar

1½ cups water

1 cinnamon stick

1 or 2 whole cloves

2½ cups bottled cranberry juice

1 tablespoon orange- or cranberry-flavored vodka, or plain vodka

1 tablespoon light corn syrup

Makes about 1 quart (1 liter)

Peaches Bellini Sorbet

If you are lucky enough to come upon local peaches that
are exceptionally sweet, reduce the sugar by a couple of
tablespoons. Otherwise, keep in mind if you taste the peach
base before freezing that the cold will diminish the effect of
the sugar.

1 In a food processor or blender, puree the peaches with the cold
   water until smooth. Pour into a large bowl.

2 Stir in the sugar, lemon juice, peach brandy, and corn syrup. If you
   have time, cover and refrigerate the peach puree for 1 to 2 hours
   to allow the flavors to develop.

3 Whisk the puree to blend. Pour into the canister of an ice cream
   maker and freeze according to the manufacturer's directions.
   Transfer the sorbet to a covered container and freeze until it is firm
   enough to scoop, at least 3 hours or overnight.

4 To serve, scoop the sorbet into 4 to 6 chilled wide-mouthed
   champagne coupes or wine glasses. Pour some of the sparkling
   wine over each and serve at once. Note: A "split" (375 ml) of
   sparkling wine will be plenty for this recipe. Prosecco, which
   is traditional for a Bellini, only comes in larger bottles. A good
   solution: drink all that's left over.

INGREDIENTS

1½ pounds (675 grams,
   about 4 to 6 medium)
   ripe peaches, peeled
   and pitted, or 3 cups
   frozen unsweetened peach
   slices, thawed

¼ cup cold water

1 cup sugar

1 tablespoon fresh
   lemon juice

1 tablespoon peach brandy
   or vodka

1 tablespoon light corn syrup

1 bottle (750 ml) Prosecco
   or other dry but fruity
   sparkling wine, well chilled

Makes about 3½ cups

COOL TIPS FOR SUCCESS

Chilling the ice cream base in
the refrigerator prior to freezing
allows time for the flavors to
blend, shortens the processing
time in your ice cream machine,
and improves the texture of the
finished product.

Pomegranate Martini Sorbet

The wildly popular sweet-tart drink is here transformed into a fabulous ice, perfect to serve as a dessert or as a palate cleanser between courses at a long meal. Or pack it into a tall glass and add a straw.

1 In a small saucepan, combine the sugar and water. Cook over medium heat, stirring often, until the sugar dissolves. Boil the syrup without stirring for 3 minutes, or until reduced to ¾ cup.

2 Pour the sugar syrup into a heatproof medium bowl. Stir in the pomegranate juice, orange juice, gin, corn syrup, and salt. Cover and refrigerate for 3 hours, or until very cold.

3 Pour the pomegranate base into the canister of an ice cream maker. Freeze according to the manufacturer's directions. Transfer the sorbet to a covered container and freeze until it is firm enough to scoop, at least 3 hours or overnight. To serve, scoop the sorbet into 4 to 6 chilled, wide-mouthed champagne coupes, wine glasses, or dessert dishes. Sprinkle the pomegranate seeds on top.

INGREDIENTS

1 cup sugar

¾ cup water

2 cups unsweetened pomegranate juice

1½ tablespoons fresh orange or lemon juice

1½ tablespoons gin or vodka

1 tablespoon light corn syrup

Dash of salt

Seeds of 1 fresh pomegranate, for garnish (optional)

Makes about 3 cups

Watermelon-Raspberry Sorbet

Make this in the heat of summer, when fruits are inexpensive and laden with sweet juices. Plain watermelon sorbets often look a bit anemic, but a small infusion of raspberry intensifies both the appearance and flavor. Pressing the fruits through a sieve ensures a smooth texture. Garnish each serving with a few fresh raspberries or watermelon chunks, if you like.

1 Combine the sugar and water in a small saucepan. Cook over medium heat, stirring often, until the sugar dissolves. Boil the syrup without stirring for 2 minutes. Remove from the heat and let cool.

2 In a blender or food processor, combine the watermelon chunks, raspberries, lemon juice, vodka, and salt. Pour in the sugar syrup and puree until smooth.

3 Strain the watermelon puree into a bowl, pressing through as much of the fruit solids as possible. Cover and refrigerate the puree until very cold, at least 2 hours or as long as 2 days.

4 Stir the mixture to blend and pour into the canister of an ice cream maker. Freeze according to the manufacturer's directions. Transfer the sorbet to a covered container and freeze until firm enough to scoop, at least 3 hours or overnight.

INGREDIENTS

¾ cup sugar

1 cup water

2½ pounds (1 kg) watermelon, rind and seeds discarded, flesh cut into chunks (about 4 cups)

½ cup fresh raspberries

1½ tablespoons fresh lemon juice

1 tablespoon raspberry vodka or plain vodka

Dash of salt

Makes about 1 quart (1 liter)

Blood Orange–Ginger Sorbet

This citrus-based sorbet can be made with Valencia or navel oranges, of course, but you shouldn't miss out on the vibrant jolt of color when blood oranges are available. In addition, the undercurrent of ginger adds a zesty bite to the sweet ice.

1 Combine the sugar, water, ginger, and orange zest in a small saucepan. Cook over medium heat, stirring often, until the sugar dissolves. Boil the syrup without stirring for 2 minutes. Remove from the heat, cover, and let steep at room temperature for 30 minutes.

2 Strain the syrup into a bowl and discard the ginger and orange zest. Stir in the orange juice, corn syrup, and vodka. Cover and refrigerate for 2 hours, or until very cold.

3 Pour into the canister of an ice cream maker. Freeze according to the manufacturer's directions. Transfer to a covered container and freeze until firm, at least 3 hours or overnight.

INGREDIENTS

1 cup sugar

1 cup water

¼ cup peeled and coarsely chopped fresh ginger (about 1½ ounces or 35 grams)

3 strips of blood orange zest (each about ½-inch wide and 2 inches long, or 1¼-cm wide and 5 cm long)

1 cup blood orange juice (from 4 to 5 blood oranges)

3 tablespoons light corn syrup

1 tablespoon orange-flavored vodka, plain vodka, or orange liqueur

Makes about 3 cups

Mocha Midnight Sorbet

Since this dark sorbet is made exclusively with cocoa powder and contains no solid chocolate, there is very little fat in the form of cocoa butter and no added fat at all in this immensely satisfying dessert. Dark with a distinct illusion of richness, this sorbet will surely satisfy any chocolate lover.

1 In a medium saucepan, combine the sugar, cocoa powder, and salt. Whisk to blend. Gradually mix in the water and espresso or coffee. Whisk in the corn syrup until well blended.

2 Cook over medium heat, whisking frequently, for 3 to 5 minutes, or until the sugar dissolves and the liquid is smooth. Remove from the heat and set aside to cool to room temperature. Then stir in the vanilla, cover, and refrigerate for 2 hours or until cold.

3 Whisk briefly to blend, then pour into the canister of an ice cream maker. Freeze according to the manufacturer's directions. Transfer the sorbet to a covered container and freeze until it is firm enough to scoop, at least 3 hours or overnight.

INGREDIENTS

1½ cups sugar

¾ cup Dutch process unsweetened cocoa powder

⅛ teaspoon salt

2 cups water

1 cup brewed espresso or strong coffee

1 tablespoon light corn syrup

½ teaspoon vanilla extract

Makes about 1 quart (1 liter)

Chocolate Granita

This excellent chocolate ice requires no machine, just a little extra time.

1 In a medium saucepan, combine the sugar, water, and cocoa powder. Cook over medium heat, whisking, until the sugar dissolves and the mixture is well blended. Transfer to a bowl and let cool to room temperature. Stir in the chocolate syrup, cover, and refrigerate until very cold, at least 2 hours.

2 Pour the chocolate syrup into a shallow 8- or 9-inch (20- or 23-cm) square metal baking pan and cover with plastic wrap. Freeze for 45 minutes, or until the granita is frozen around the edges and the surface is covered with a thin layer of ice. Using a fork, break up the ice, scraping the ice crystals from the edges of the pan and mixing them into the center to distribute evenly.

3 Return the pan, covered, to the freezer for about 30 minutes, or until the edges have frozen again. Repeat the process at least 3 more times, scraping, mixing, and re-freezing until large, granular ice crystals have formed and the mixture is light and slightly slushy. Do not let the granita harden into a solid mass. Serve at once or cover and freeze for up to 4 hours.

INGREDIENTS

½ cup sugar

3 cups water

1 tablespoon unsweetened cocoa powder

⅓ cup Chocolate Syrup, homemade (page 179) or store-bought

Makes about 1 quart (1 liter)

VARIATION

Chocolate Ice: Prepare the chocolate syrup as in Step 1 and refrigerate until cold. Whisk to blend and pour into the canister of an ice cream maker. Freeze according to the manufacturer's directions, until the mixture is frozen and spoonable but not hard or crumbly. Serve at once, or transfer to a covered container and freeze for about 30 minutes before serving.

Espresso Granita

That espresso is the most classic of granita flavors should come as no surprise, since the coarse-crystalled ice originated in Italy. It's a frozen dessert you can make with no machine, and the effect is appreciably different from a standard sorbet. Serve with biscotti or amaretti.

1 In a medium bowl, combine the hot espresso and sugar. Stir to dissolve the sugar. Let cool to room temperature. Cover and refrigerate until very cold, at least 2 hours.

2 Pour into a shallow 8-inch (20-cm) square pan and cover with plastic. Freeze for 45 minutes, or until the granita is frozen around the edges and the surface is covered with a thin layer of ice. Using a fork, break up the ice, scraping the ice crystals from the edges of the pan and mixing them into the center to distribute evenly.

3 Return the pan, covered, to the freezer for about 30 minutes, or until the edges have frozen again. Repeat the process at least 3 more times, scraping, mixing, and re-freezing until large, granular ice crystals have formed and the mixture is light and slightly slushy. Do not let the granita harden into a solid mass. Serve at once, or cover and freeze for 1 to 4 hours.

INGREDIENTS

2 cups freshly brewed espresso or very strong coffee

¼ cup sugar

Makes about 3 cups

VARIATIONS

Café Latte Granita: Add 1 cup of milk to the espresso mixture in Step 1.

Espresso Ice: Here's the same base processed in an ice cream maker. Refrigerate the espresso mixture until cold as directed in Step 1. Pour into the canister of an ice cream maker. Freeze according to the manufacturer's directions, until the mixture is frozen and spoonable. Serve at once or transfer to a covered container and freeze for 30 minutes before serving.

"a hot fudge sundae and a trashy
novel is my idea
of heaven."

–Barbara Walters

sundaes
& parfaits

Warm Amaretto-Peach Sundae

This is a chic, unstructured sundae that incorporates a classic Italian dessert—baked fresh peaches stuffed with an intense almond filling—with a fresh peach's favorite companion: raspberry sauce. You can make it easy by forming these sundaes with purchased ice cream.

1 Preheat the oven to 350°F (180°C). Spread out the almonds in an even layer in a small baking pan. Toast in the oven, stirring once or twice, for 7 to 9 minutes, or until lightly browned and fragrant. Transfer to a dish and set aside to cool. Leave the oven on. Reserve half of the toasted almonds for garnish; finely chop the remaining ¼ cup.

2 Generously grease a 2-quart (2-liter) baking dish with the butter. Cut 1 peach in half through its stem end. Twist the halves in opposite directions to separate and free them from the pit. Repeat with remaining peaches. Place the peach halves, cut-sides up, in the prepared dish and drizzle with 1 tablespoon of the amaretto.

3 In a medium bowl, combine the chopped almonds with the remaining 1 tablespoon amaretto, the crushed amaretti, the brown sugar, egg yolk, and salt. Mix with a fork until well blended. Stuff the hollow of each peach with an equal amount of the almond filling, mounding it slightly to resemble a peach pit.

4 Bake for 20 to 25 minutes, or until the topping is crisp and browned and the peaches are softened but still hold their shape. Baste the peaches with any juices from the baking dish.

5 To serve, drizzle about 3 tablespoons of Raspberry Sauce onto each of 6 dessert plates or shallow bowls. Place 1 warm peach half on each. Add 1 or 2 scoops of ice cream on the side, sprinkle the reserved toasted almonds on top, and serve at once.

INGREDIENTS

½ cup sliced almonds

1 tablespoon unsalted butter

3 ripe but firm peaches, preferably freestone

2 tablespoons amaretto liqueur

½ cup coarsely crumbled amaretti (crisp Italian almond macaroons, such as Lazzaroni® brand)

¼ cup (packed) dark brown sugar

1 egg yolk

Dash of salt

¾ cup Raspberry Sauce (page 66)

1 quart Tahitian Double Vanilla Ice Cream (page 12), Fresh Peach Ice Cream (page 14), or store-bought vanilla or peach ice cream

Serves 6

Butterscotch-Pecan Sundae

Easy, gooey, and sweet, this classic sundae offers a tempting alternative to hot fudge. Fresh pecans will make all the difference to the sauce.

1 Place a scoop of ice cream in each of 4 tall sundae glasses. Ladle 3 to 4 tablespoons of the Butterscotch-Pecan Sauce over the ice cream. Repeat with the remaining ice cream and most of the sauce.

2 Top each sundae with a dollop of whipped cream and garnish with a few pecan pieces from the sauce.

Butterscotch-Pecan Sauce

1 Preheat the oven to 350°F (180 °C). Spread out the pecans in a small baking pan. Toast in the oven for 7 to 10 minutes, stirring once or twice, until lightly browned and fragrant. Transfer to a dish and set aside to cool.

2 In a small saucepan, combine the brown sugar, corn syrup, cream, butter, and salt. Bring to a boil over medium heat, stirring frequently. Reduce the heat to medium-low and cook for 10 to 15 minutes longer, or until the sauce has thickened and reduced to about 1½ cups. Remove from the heat and set aside to cool for about 30 minutes. Stir in the vanilla and the toasted pecans. Cover and refrigerate for up to 1 week. Serve at room temperature or barely warm.

INGREDIENTS

1½ pints (675 ml) No-Cook Vanilla Ice Cream (page 25), or store-bought vanilla ice cream

Butterscotch-Pecan Sauce (recipe follows)

Whipped cream, for garnish

Makes 4

Butterscotch-Pecan Sauce

½ cup pecan halves and pieces

1 cup (packed) light brown sugar

½ cup light corn syrup

½ cup heavy cream

4 tablespoons unsalted butter, cut into pieces

Dash of salt

1 teaspoon vanilla extract

Makes about 1½ cups

VARIATION

Butterscotch Sauce: For plain butterscotch sauce, simply omit the pecans and skip to Step 2.

Peach Melba Coupe

Peach Melba is a classic ice cream dessert served in stemmed glasses with wide bowls called coupes. You can also dice the peaches and layer the dessert into tall narrow glasses and call it a parfait. To turn this into an "almost-instant" dessert, simply use canned or frozen peaches and skip Steps 1 and 2.

1 Dip the peaches into a saucepan of boiling water for 10 to 30 seconds to loosen the skins. Lift out with a slotted spoon and rinse under cold running water. Slip off the skins. Halve the peaches and remove the pits.

2 In a medium saucepan, combine the sugar, water, lemon zest, cinnamon stick, and cloves. Bring to a boil, stirring to dissolve the sugar. Reduce the heat to low and simmer for 5 minutes. Add the peach halves and poach, turning gently once so they cook evenly, until they are barely tender, about 10 minutes. Remove from the heat and let the peaches cool in the syrup, then cover and refrigerate until chilled. (The peaches can be poached up to a day in advance.)

3 Drain the peaches and cut them into slices.

4 To assemble the parfaits, choose 4 large-stemmed wine glasses or tall, narrow, straight-sided parfait dishes. Put a small scoop of vanilla ice cream in the bottom of each glass. Add a layer of peaches, using about half. Drizzle on half the Raspberry Sauce. Repeat with more ice cream and the remaining peaches and sauce. Top with a small dollop or swirl of whipped cream, if you like, and garnish with whole berries or chopped almonds. Serve at once.

INGREDIENTS

3   ripe peaches

¾   cup sugar

1   cup water

1   strip of lemon zest

1   cinnamon stick
(3 inches or 7½ cm long)

2   whole cloves

1   pint Tahitian Double Vanilla
Ice Cream (page 12),
or your favorite
premium brand

Raspberry Sauce (page 66)

Sweetened whipped cream, for garnish (optional)

Chopped toasted almonds or whole berries, for garnish

Serves 4

Brandied Fruit Parfait

These parfaits are perfectly suited to holiday entertaining, or to any wintry evening that calls for a festive dessert, because they can be completely assembled a day in advance. If you have extra angelica after making the chutney, use a small leaf-shaped cookie cutter to form holly leaves as a garnish for each serving. Otherwise, decorate the parfaits with cinnamon sticks.

1 In a heavy 1-quart (1-liter) nonreactive saucepan, combine the Brandied Fruit Sauce, orange juice, brown sugar, orange zest and juice, bourbon, and cinnamon. Bring to a boil over medium heat, stirring to dissolve the sugar. Reduce the heat to medium-low and cook, stirring occasionally, for 5 to 10 minutes, or until the sauce thickens. Stir in the cream until well blended.

2 Transfer the sauce into a heatproof bowl and let cool completely. Use at once, or cover and refrigerate for up to 4 days.

3 To assemble the parfaits, spoon about 1 tablespoon of the brandied fruit into the bottom of each of 4 parfait glasses. Add 1 scoop of ice cream to each and top with about 3 tablespoons of sauce. Repeat with 1 more scoop of ice cream and the remaining sauce. Cover each parfait with plastic wrap and freeze until firm, at least 4 hours or overnight.

4 About 15 minutes before serving, transfer the parfaits from the freezer to the refrigerator to soften slightly. Discard the plastic wrap and top each parfait with whipped cream and a light dusting of nutmeg. Serve at once.

INGREDIENTS

1 cup Brandied Fruit Sauce (page 187), or good quality store-bought all-fruit mincemeat

¾ cup orange juice

⅔ cup dark brown sugar

Finely grated zest and juice from 1 orange

¼ cup bourbon, brandy, or dark rum

½ teaspoon ground cinnamon

3 tablespoons heavy cream

1½ pints (675 ml) Cinnamon-Basil Ice Cream (page 18), or store-bought eggnog, cinnamon, or vanilla ice cream

Whipped cream and freshly grated nutmeg, for garnish

Serves 4

Frozen Yogurt Berry Parfait with Cinnamon-Nut Crunch

When cereal is toasted with sweetened nuts, it makes a delicious cinnamon "crunch" similar to granola and ideal for layering in parfaits.

1 In a large skillet, melt the butter over medium heat. Add the cereal, sugar, honey, and almonds. Cook, stirring frequently, for 4 to 5 minutes or until the sugar dissolves and the mixture is lightly toasted and caramelized. Stir in the cinnamon. Spread on a foil-lined baking sheet and set aside to cool completely. Use your fingers to break up the cinnamon-nut crunch into small clusters.

2 To assemble the parfaits, place 1 scoop of frozen yogurt in the bottom of each of 4 parfait glasses. Top each with ¼ cup of the berries and ¼ cup of the cinnamon-nut crunch. Add another scoop of yogurt and repeat the layers by adding the remaining berries and ending with a layer of crunch. Serve at once.

INGREDIENTS

1 tablespoon unsalted butter

1½ cups corn or wheat flake cereal, crushed into coarse crumbs

1 tablespoon sugar

1 tablespoon honey

½ cup sliced almonds, chopped walnuts, or chopped pecans

1 teaspoon ground cinnamon

1 quart (1 liter) raspberry frozen yogurt, or frozen yogurt or ice cream flavor of your choice

2 cups assorted fresh berries, such as raspberries, blackberries, blueberries, and sliced strawberries

Serves 4

Roast Banana Split
with Mixed Berries

Here's a new twist on an old favorite, the banana split. All the bells and whistles included here were inspired by a roasted banana split sundae served at a California eatery that was popular in my youth, Rosalie's. While hot banana, baked in its skin, makes for a pleasing contrast to the cold ice cream, plain sliced raw banana is much more attractive. Please note: Both sauces should be made before starting to assemble the sundaes.

1 Place 4 dinner-size plates in the freezer. If desired, scoop out 4 servings each of vanilla and chocolate ice cream and return them to the freezer until serving time.

2 If you choose to roast the bananas, preheat the oven to 350°F (180 °C). Place the bananas in their peels on a foil-lined baking sheet. Bake for 15 to 20 minutes, or until the skins turn black and the fruit is warm throughout. When cool enough to handle, cut each banana in half lengthwise and remove the peel. Otherwise, simply peel the raw bananas and split them lengthwise in half.

3 To assemble the banana splits, arrange 2 banana halves in each chilled dish. Working quickly, place a scoop of vanilla on one end of the plate and a scoop of chocolate on the opposite. Pile ½ cup berries in the center. Drizzle the Caramel Sauce over the vanilla ice cream and the Chocolate-Nut Sauce over the chocolate ice cream. Add a dollop of whipped cream and garnish with a mint sprig. Serve at once.

INGREDIENTS

4   firm but ripe bananas, in their skins

1   pint (450 ml) Tahitian Double Vanilla Ice Cream (page 12), or your favorite premium brand

1   pint (450 ml) Chocolate Custard Ice Cream (page 30), or your favorite premium brand

2   cups fresh berries (raspberries, blackberries, hulled and quartered strawberries, and/or blueberries)

Caramel Sauce (page 185)

Chocolate-Nut Sauce (page 184)

Sweetened whipped cream, for garnish

4   small sprigs of mint, for garnish

Serves 4

...berry Sundae

If you make the Strawberry Dream Light Ice Cream with fresh berries, these pretty pink sundaes are best enjoyed during the summer months. Otherwise, with frozen strawberries, you can serve them all year round.

1 Put 4 scoops of strawberry ice cream in each of 4 tall sundae glasses. Spoon 2 tablespoons Simple Strawberry Sauce over each. Add another scoop and the remaining sauce.

2 Top the sundaes with a dollop or swirl of whipped cream and garnish with a fresh strawberry.

Simple Strawberry Sauce

1 Working in batches if needed, puree the frozen berries with their juices in a food processor or blender until smooth. Transfer to a bowl and stir in the lemon juice and 2 tablespoons of the sugar. Set aside for 2 or 3 minutes to allow the sugar to dissolve.

2 If you're adding a liqueur, stir it in. Taste the sauce and add the remaining 1 tablespoon sugar if you think it's needed. Use at once, or cover and refrigerate for up to 2 days.

INGREDIENTS

1½ pints (675 ml) Strawberry Dream Light Ice Cream (page 46), or your favorite premium strawberry ice cream

Simple Strawberry Sauce (recipe follows)

Whipped cream, for garnish

4 whole strawberries, for garnish

Makes 4

Simple Strawberry Sauce

1 bag (1 pound or 450 grams) unsweetened frozen strawberries, partially thawed, juices reserved

2 teaspoons fresh lemon juice

2 to 3 tablespoons sugar, to taste

1 tablespoon Grand Marnier or framboise (optional)

Makes about 1 cup

Sticky Toffee Sundae

Sticky toffee pudding is one of Britain's greatest contributions to modern culture. The word *pudding* in England simply means a sweet. In this case, it's a sweet moist date cake topped with toffee. Here, a scoop of ice cream transforms the "pudding" into a fabulous sundae. This dessert is rich, so serve small portions to begin.

1 In a heavy medium saucepan, combine the dates and water. Bring to a boil over medium heat. Remove from the heat, stir in the baking soda, and let stand for about 30 minutes.

2 Preheat the oven to 325°F (160°C). Generously grease a 9-inch (23-cm) square baking pan. Line the bottom with waxed paper.

3 In a large bowl, beat the butter and brown sugar with an electric mixer for 3 to 5 minutes, or until light and very fluffy. Add the eggs, one at a time, beating well after each addition. Beat in the vanilla. With a wooden spoon or rubber spatula, mix in the flour and baking powder. Add the date mixture and mix just until well blended. Turn the batter into the prepared baking pan.

4 Bake the sticky toffee pudding for 40 to 45 minutes, or until the cake is just beginning to pull away from the sides of the pan and a toothpick inserted into the center comes out with a moist crumb. Remove the pan from the oven. Using a toothpick, poke holes all over the top of the cake and drizzle with about ¾ cup of the warm Toffee Sauce. Let cool in the pan on a wire rack for at least 30 minutes before cutting into squares or rectangles. Serve the "pudding" warm or at room temperature.

5 To assemble the dessert, place a piece of sticky toffee pudding on each of 6 or 8 dessert plates or in shallow bowls. Top with a large scoop of ice cream and drizzle warm Toffee Sauce over all.

INGREDIENTS

8   ounces (225 grams) chopped pitted dates (about 1½ cups)

1¼ cups water

1   teaspoon baking soda

4   tablespoons unsalted butter, softened

¾   cup (packed) dark brown sugar

2   eggs

1½ teaspoons vanilla extract

1¾ cups all-purpose flour

1   teaspoon baking powder

1½ pints (675 ml) Tahitian Double Vanilla Ice Cream (page 12), or your favorite premium brand

Toffee Sauce (page 185)

Serves 6 to 8

Fudge Brownie Sundae

Rich, fudgy brownies layered with vanilla ice cream and topped off with an intense bittersweet chocolate sauce can go from casual to dressy, depending upon your dishes. Of course, you can always make it easy by simply purchasing the brownies.

1 Preheat the oven to 350°F (180°C). Generously grease an 8-inch (20-cm) square baking pan. Dust with flour; shake out the excess.

2 Place a large heatproof bowl over a pot of barely simmering water. Add the chocolate and butter and cook over low heat, stirring, until melted and smooth. Remove from the heat and set aside to cool for 5 minutes.

3 Whisk in the sugar. Add the eggs and vanilla and beat until well blended. Add the flour and salt and stir until just blended. Turn the batter into the prepared pan.

4 Bake the brownies for 30 minutes, or until a toothpick inserted 2 inches (5 cm) from the edge comes out with small, moist crumbs. Do not overbake. Cool on a wire rack for 20 to 30 minutes. Cut into squares. Serve at once, or wrap well and refrigerate for up to 3 days; freeze for longer storage.

5 To assemble the sundaes, place 1 brownie square in each of 8 large goblets, tall glasses, or dessert dishes. Top with a scoop of ice cream. Repeat with a second brownie and more ice cream. Drizzle 2 or 3 tablespoons of barely warm Bittersweet Fudge Sauce over each sundae. To complete the picture, top each sundae, if you like, with a dollop of whipped cream and a maraschino cherry. Serve at once.

INGREDIENTS

4 ounces (100 grams) unsweetened chocolate, finely chopped

1 stick (4 ounces or 100 grams) unsalted butter, cut into pieces

1½ cups sugar

3 eggs, lightly beaten

1½ teaspoons vanilla extract

¾ cup all-purpose flour

¼ teaspoon salt

1 quart (1 liter) Tahitian Double Vanilla Ice Cream (page 12), or the flavor of your choice

Bittersweet Fudge Sauce (page 184)

Whipped cream and maraschino cherries, for garnish (optional)

Serves 8

Haute Fudge Sundae

There's a reason a recipe becomes a classic. In both flavor and texture, this is simply one of the best combinations of ice cream and sauce ever conceived. For the full effect, the dessert must be served in old-fashioned, soda-fountain sundae glasses.

1 Place a scoop of ice cream in each of 4 tall sundae glasses. Ladle 2 or 3 tablespoons of Haute Fudge Sauce over the ice cream. Repeat with the remaining ice cream and more sauce.

2 Top each sundae with a dollop or swirl of whipped cream and garnish with a sprinkling of chopped walnuts and a single cherry.

Haute Fudge Sauce

1 In a heavy nonreactive medium saucepan, combine the cream, brown sugar, cocoa powder, corn syrup, and salt. Cook over low heat, whisking often, for 5 minutes, or until the sugar dissolves and bubbles appear on the surface. Remove from the heat.

2 Add the chopped chocolate and the butter to the hot chocolate cream. Whisk until melted and smooth. Stir in the vanilla.

3 Use the fudge sauce at once or let cool to room temperature. If made in advance, refrigerate in a covered jar for up to 1 week.

INGREDIENTS

1½ pints (675 ml) Tahitian Double Vanilla Ice Cream (page 12), or your favorite premium brand

Haute Fudge Sauce (recipe follows)

Whipped cream, for garnish

¼ cup chopped toasted walnuts, for garnish (optional)

4 maraschino cherries, for garnish

Serves 4

Haute Fudge Sauce

½ cup heavy cream

1 cup (packed) dark brown sugar

½ cup Dutch process unsweetened cocoa powder

¼ cup light corn syrup

Dash of salt

2 ounces (50 grams) bittersweet or semisweet chocolate, finely chopped

2 tablespoons unsalted butter, cut into pieces

1 teaspoon vanilla extract

Makes about 1½ cups

Candy Cane Sundae with Peppermint Fudge Sauce

It's Christmas in July or ice cream for Christmas, depending upon when you choose to serve these charming sundaes, which will delight a younger crowd. Hard peppermint candies are a favorite year 'round, but during the holidays you may want to use the miniature candy canes available in supermarkets and discount stores. When crushed, either of these small candies equals about 1 tablespoon.

1 Unwrap all the candies. If using candy canes, set 4 aside for garnish. Place the other 4 in a heavy-duty plastic bag and crush into small pieces with a rolling pin or the bottom of a pot. Avoid smashing them to a powder. There will be about ¼ cup crushed candy.

2 Place 2 scoops of vanilla ice cream in each of 4 sundae glasses or dessert dishes. Drizzle about ¼ cup of warm Peppermint Fudge Sauce over each serving of ice cream and top with 1 tablespoon of the crushed candy. If using candy canes, use 1 of the remaining candies to garnish each sundae. Serve at once.

Peppermint Fudge Sauce

1 In a heatproof medium bowl, combine the chocolate, butter, water, corn syrup, vanilla, peppermint extract, and salt. Set over a pan of barely simmering water and stir constantly until the chocolate and butter are melted and the sauce is smooth.

2 Use the sauce at once, or transfer to a container and let cool; then cover and refrigerate for up to 1 week.

INGREDIENTS

4   hard peppermint candies, or 8 miniature (2-inch or 5-cm) candy canes

1   quart (1 liter) Tahitian Double Vanilla Ice Cream (page 12), or your favorite premium brand

Peppermint Fudge Sauce (recipe follows)

Serves 4

Peppermint Fudge Sauce

8   ounces (225 grams) bittersweet chocolate, chopped

4   tablespoons unsalted butter, cut into pieces

¼   cup water

¼   cup light corn syrup

½   teaspoon vanilla extract

¼   teaspoon peppermint extract

Dash of salt

Makes 1 cup

Black and White Chocolate Cups

More of a refined dessert than a soda fountain sundae, these charming ice cream–filled cups provide the perfect finish to an elegant dinner party.

1 Line 10 muffin or cupcake tins with paper liners. Place the chocolate in a heatproof bowl placed over a pan of barely simmering water. Cook over low heat, stirring occasionally, until melted and smooth. Remove the chocolate from the heat and set aside for 5 to 10 minutes to cool and thicken slightly.

2 Spoon 1 tablespoon of the melted chocolate into each paper liner. Using a narrow pastry brush, spread the chocolate over the bottom and up the sides of the liners to coat evenly, leaving a ⅛-inch (⅓-cm) margin at the top. Freeze for 30 minutes or until the chocolate is firm. Set the bowl of chocolate aside.

3 When the cups are set, return the bowl of chocolate to the pan of barely simmering water. Add 1 more tablespoon of warm chocolate to each cup and brush over the bottom and up the sides of the paper liner, forming a second layer, still leaving the bare margin at the top. Refrigerate or freeze for at least 1 hour.

4 To remove the chocolate from each paper liner, grasp the top edges of the paper and gently peel it away from the chocolate; set on a parchment-lined baking sheet. Do not rush this process, as the cups are fragile. Refrigerate or freeze until the chocolate is firm; then cover and refrigerate until needed.

5 To serve, carefully set a frozen chocolate cup on each dessert plate. Fill with a scoop of White Chocolate Ice Cream (made without the Bittersweet Fudge Ripple, if desired). Top with a dollop of Chocolate Whipped Cream and garnish with a single berry or crystallized violet.

INGREDIENTS

12 ounces (350 grams) semisweet or white chocolate, chopped

1 quart (1 liter) White Chocolate Ice Cream (page 26), Tahitian Double Vanilla Ice Cream (page 12), or your favorite premium brand

Chocolate Whipped Cream (page 185), for garnish

Fresh raspberries or crystallized violets, for garnish

Serves 8 to 10

Ethereal Coffee Sundae

What makes this sundae ethereal is Blum's Coffee Crunch, a melt-in-your-mouth candy topping that's sprinkled on at the last moment.

1 Place a scoop of ice cream in each of 4 tall sundae glasses. Ladle about 2 tablespoons of the Maple-Bathed Walnuts over the ice cream. Repeat with the remaining ice cream and walnuts.

2 Cap each sundae with a dollop or swirl of whipped cream and sprinkle 1 to 2 tablespoons of the Coffee Crunch on top.

Blum's Coffee Crunch

1 Coat a jellyroll pan or other large baking sheet with nonstick cooking spray, or line with a silicone liner.

2 In a 2½- to 3-quart (2½- to 3-liter) saucepan, combine the sugar, espresso, and corn syrup. Bring to a simmer over medium-low heat, stirring to dissolve the sugar. Increase the heat to medium-high. Boil without stirring until the syrup reaches 290°F (145°C).

3 Remove the pan from the heat and let the boiling subside, then add the baking soda. The syrup will bubble up to about 4 times its original volume. Use a long-handled whisk to incorporate the baking soda. While it is still hot and liquid, pour onto the prepared jellyroll pan. Leave the big bubbling mass on the baking sheet—it will shrink a bit as it cools.

4 Let the candy stand uncovered at room temperature for 30 to 40 minutes, or until completely cool. Lift it off of the pan and crack into 3 or 4 pieces. Immediately place each chunk in a heavy-duty plastic zippered bag to prevent it from becoming sticky. Just before serving, crush the crunch into irregular bite-size chunks.

INGREDIENTS

1½ pints (675 ml) Coffee Ice Cream (page 32) or your favorite flavor

Maple-Bathed Walnuts (page 186) or Easy Chocolate Sauce (page 184)

Whipped cream, for garnish

Blum's Coffee Crunch, for garnish (recipe follows)

Makes 4

Blum's Coffee Crunch

1½ cups sugar

¼ cup brewed espresso or strong coffee

¼ cup light corn syrup

1 tablespoon baking soda, sifted

Makes about 3 cups

Tiramisu Parfait

To form these charming individual desserts, you'll need four freezer-safe glasses (6 to 8 ounces, or 175 to 225 grams, each), such as Irish coffee mugs, bistro glasses, or individual soufflé molds.

1 Combine the sugar and water in a small saucepan. Cook over medium heat, stirring often, until the sugar dissolves. Boil the syrup without stirring for 2 minutes. Remove from the heat and let cool to room temperature. Stir in the Cognac and coffee.

2 Pour half the coffee syrup into a wide shallow bowl. Add half the ladyfingers and turn them until they have absorbed all of the liquid. Repeat with the remaining syrup and ladyfingers.

3 To assemble the parfaits: Let the ice cream stand at room temperature for 10 to 15 minutes to soften. Working quickly, arrange alternating layers of ice cream and ladyfingers, trimmed to fit, in the parfait glasses, filling them about ¾ full. Cover tightly and freeze for at least 2 hours and up to 5 days.

4 To serve, remove the parfaits from the freezer about 10 minutes before serving to allow them to soften slightly. Top each with a dollop of whipped cream and a dusting of cocoa powder.

INGREDIENTS

⅓ cup sugar

⅓ cup water

3 tablespoons Cognac, brandy, or rum

3 tablespoons double-strength brewed coffee or 1 tablespoon instant espresso powder dissolved in 3 tablespoons boiling water

10 to 12 whole soft ladyfingers or fingers of sponge cake

1 pint (450 ml) Coffee Ice Cream (page 32), or your favorite premium brand

Whipped cream, for garnish

Cocoa powder, for dusting

Serves 4

COOL TIPS FOR SUCCESS

"Flash freezing" composed ice cream desserts will keep your garnishes intact. Simply freeze the completed dessert uncovered until the surface is firm to the touch, then wrap airtight.

Baked Potato Sundae

People are enchanted by whimsical desserts that trick the eye, what the French call *trompe l'oeil*. This pseudo spud is perfect for April Fool's Day or St. Patrick's Day . . . or anytime you want to elicit a smile or two from your guests, especially some young ones.

INGREDIENTS

1 quart (1 liter) Tahitian Double Vanilla Ice Cream (page 12), or your favorite premium brand, softened slightly

1 cup sweet ground chocolate and cocoa (such as Ghirardelli brand) or other sweetened cocoa powder

20 pine nuts (about 1½ teaspoons)

2 cups marshmallow cream or whipped cream

2 tablespoons chocolate-covered toffee bits

2 teaspoons green decors (also called candy sprinkles or jimmies)

1 to 2 cups Easy Chocolate Sauce (page 184), or your favorite store-bought chocolate sauce or syrup

Serves 4

1 Have ready 4 sheets of plastic wrap about 10 inches (25 cm) long. Place 2 or 3 scoops of ice cream side by side on each sheet and enclose in the plastic, wrapping them airtight. Use your hands to squeeze and mold each batch of ice cream into a smooth, irregular oval resembling a large potato. Freeze the 4 "potatoes" for at least 2 hours, or until firm.

2 Place the chocolate and cocoa in a large shallow bowl. Working with one "potato" at a time, unwrap the ice cream. Use the tip of a teaspoon to make a few realistic indentations on the surface, then roll in the cocoa to coat completely. Place in a baking pan or a deep plastic container large enough to hold all the "potatoes." Repeat with the remaining ice cream. Insert 5 pine nuts, randomly spaced, into each potato to resemble sprouting eyes. Cover and freeze for at least 2 hours or until firm. Reserve any leftover cocoa for touch-ups.

3 If any ice cream is visible on the "potatoes," roll in cocoa again to cover. Place 1 "potato" on each of 4 chilled dessert plates. Working quickly, draw a knife lengthwise down the center of each "potato," making an indentation ¾ to 1 inch (2 to 2½ cm) deep. Gently press both ends, as if opening a baked potato to expose the inside. Top each with a large dollop of marshmallow cream (to resemble sour cream). Scatter toffee bits (for bacon bits) over the top and sprinkle with green decors (for chives). Drizzle chocolate sauce on each plate, or pass at the table. Serve at once.

"in my films, all the great things are put together. it's not like one kind of ice cream, but rather a very big sundae."

–film director George Lucas

ice cream cakes, molded desserts, & pies

Baby Baked Alaskas

Great for entertaining, these meringue-cloaked ice cream cakes can be completely assembled a day in advance. The secret of success is to make sure your oven is up to temperature before baking them. That way, the meringue will brown before the ice cream melts.

1 Using a 3-inch (7½-cm) round cookie cutter, stamp out a circle from each slice of cake. Arrange the rounds of cake on a foil-lined baking sheet. Place a generous rounded scoop of ice cream on top of each piece of cake. Freeze for at least 30 minutes.

2 In a large bowl with an electric mixer, beat the egg whites with the cream of tartar until foamy. Gradually beat in the sugar 1 tablespoon at a time. Continue to beat the meringue until stiff glossy peaks form when the beaters are lifted.

3 Remove the ice cream–topped cakes from the freezer and, working quickly, frost each one with the meringue, spreading it on thickly and making sure to completely enclose the cake and ice cream. Return the cakes to the freezer for at least 1 hour or up to 1 day.

4 When you are ready to serve, preheat the oven to 500°F (260°C). Set the frozen sheet of desserts in the oven and bake for 3 to 5 minutes, until the edges of the meringue are browned. Serve at once.

INGREDIENTS

6 slices of vanilla pound cake, cut ½ inch (1¼ cm) thick

1 quart (1 liter) ice cream, your choice of flavor

4 egg whites

⅛ teaspoon cream of tartar

½ cup superfine sugar

Serves 6

Frozen Banana-Ginger Coconut Cream Pie

This may not be the usual banana cream pie that immediately comes to mind, but one taste and you surely won't forget it. Ginger preserves are imported from England, and sold alongside the jams and jellies at many well-stocked supermarkets. Of course, to make it easy, you may substitute a prepared graham cracker crust.

1 Preheat the oven to 350°F (180°C). Spread out the coconut evenly on a small baking sheet. Toast in the oven, stirring frequently, for 7 to 10 minutes, or until lightly browned. Transfer to a plate and let cool.

2 In a large bowl, combine the softened ice cream and ½ cup of the coconut. Using a large wooden spoon or a rubber spatula, stir in the coconut. Working quickly, gently stir in the bananas so they remain in slices and large pieces. Pile half the ice cream into the prepared crust. Dollop teaspoons of the ginger preserves randomly over the ice cream and cover with the remaining ice cream, mounding it in the center. Freeze until completely set, at least 3 hours or for up to 3 days.

3 To serve, let the pie stand in the refrigerator for 10 to 15 minutes to soften slightly. Meanwhile, in a large chilled bowl with chilled beaters, whip the heavy cream with the sugar and vanilla until stiff. Spread the whipped cream over the pie. Sprinkle the remaining ¼ cup toasted coconut on top. Use a long, sharp knife dipped in hot water and wiped dry to slice the pie into wedges.

INGREDIENTS

¾ cup shredded sweetened coconut

1½ quarts (1½ liters) Tahitian Double Vanilla Ice Cream (page 12), or your favorite premium brand, softened slightly

2 ripe bananas, peeled and sliced

9-inch (23-cm) graham cracker crumb crust, purchased or homemade (page 185), baked and chilled

½ cup ginger preserves or apricot jam, chopped if there are any large pieces

1 cup heavy cream

1 tablespoon sugar

½ teaspoon vanilla extract

Serves 6 to 8

Profiteroles

Crisp, golden cream puffs, filled with vanilla ice cream and bathed in chocolate or raspberry sauce is one of the all-time great classic desserts.

1 Preheat the oven to 400°F (200°C). In a heavy large saucepan, combine the butter, water, sugar, and salt. Bring to a boil over medium heat, stirring to melt the butter. When the water reaches a full boil and the butter is melted, add the flour all at once. Reduce the heat to medium-low and beat vigorously until the dough masses together in a ball, 1 to 2 minutes. Remove from the heat.

2 Either by hand or with an electric mixer, beat in the eggs one at a time, making sure that each egg is fully incorporated before adding the next. Continue beating until the dough is very smooth and shiny. (The dough can be mixed in a food processor, but it will not incorporate as much air.)

3 Using 2 spoons or a large pastry bag fitted with a ½-inch (1¼-cm) wide plain tip, drop 24 to 30 small mounds of dough (about ¾ inch or 2 cm in diameter) about 1½ inches (3¾ cm) apart on a buttered baking sheet.

4 Bake for 20 minutes. Reduce the oven temperature to 375°F (190°C) and bake for 5 to 10 minutes longer, or until the pastries are puffed and golden brown. Remove to a rack and let cool completely.

5 Split the cream puffs horizontally in half. Fill each with a scoop of vanilla ice cream. Set the cream puff tops in place, arrange on dessert plates, and drizzle the sauce over the profiteroles. Serve at once.

INGREDIENTS

1   stick (4 ounces or 100 grams) unsalted butter, cut into tablespoons
1   cup water
1   teaspoon sugar
½   teaspoon salt
1   cup all-purpose flour
4   large eggs
1   quart (1 liter) Tahitian Double Vanilla (page 12), or your favorite premium brand

Chocolate Ganache (page 184) or Raspberry Sauce (page 66), or both

Serves 8

Frozen Coeur à la Crème with Balsamic Strawberries

Coeur à la crème is a French dessert, made of fresh mild cheese drenched in berries, traditionally served on Valentine's Day. Here a cream cheese ice cream does the trick, drenched with balsamic-marinated strawberries.

1 In a large bowl, combine the cream cheese, milk, lemon juice, sugar, vanilla, and salt. Beat until smooth. Add the heavy cream, mixing just until well blended. Cover with plastic wrap and refrigerate for 2 hours, or until cold.

2 Pour into the canister of an ice cream maker and freeze according to the manufacturer's directions.

3 Meanwhile, line a 7- to 8-inch (17½- to 20-cm) heart-shaped mold with plastic wrap, letting the ends fall over the sides of the mold. (Alternatively, line an 8-inch [20-cm] round cake pan, or any other 1-quart [1-liter] mold.)

4 Scrape the cream cheese ice cream into the prepared mold, smoothing the top into an even layer. Wrap well and freeze for at least 2 hours, or until firm.

5 Unmold the ice cream heart onto a cold platter. Peel off the plastic wrap. Let soften in the refrigerator for about 10 minutes before serving, with the balsamic berries on the side.

Balsamic Strawberries

In a large bowl, combine the strawberries, sugar, and vinegar. Toss gently to coat. Cover and let macerate at room temperature for 30 minutes to 1 hour. If made in advance, refrigerate for up to 8 hours.

INGREDIENTS

8 ounces (225 grams) cream cheese, softened

1 cup whole milk

1 tablespoon fresh lemon juice

¾ cup sugar

1 teaspoon vanilla extract

Dash of salt

½ cup heavy cream

Balsamic Strawberries (recipe follows)

Makes about 1 quart (1 liter)

Balsamic Strawberries

3½ cups hulled, sliced strawberries (about 1 pound or 450 grams)

3 to 4 tablespoons sugar, depending upon the sweetness of the berries

1½ teaspoons balsamic vinegar

Serves 4 to 6

Ice Cream Cassata

Cassata gelata is Sicilian in origin, and its flavors are based upon the traditional Easter treat comprised of sponge cake, ricotta cheese, and lots of candied fruits and nuts. Begin this frozen version 2 days before you plan to serve it.

1 In a small jar with a tight-fitting lid, combine the candied fruits and rum. Cover and let stand at room temperature, stirring occasionally, for at least 2 hours or as long as 24 hours.

2 Trim the crusts and cut the cake lengthwise into slices ⅜ inch thick. Line a 9 by 5 by 3-inch (23 by 13 by 7½-cm) loaf pan with plastic wrap, pressing it well into the corners and letting the ends drape over the sides by at least 3 inches. Line the bottom and sides with cake slices.

3 Let the pistachio gelato stand at room temperature for 10 to 15 minutes to soften slightly. Spread it evenly over the bottom of the prepared pan, pressing gently to remove any air pockets. Cover the pan and freeze for about 2 hours, or until the gelato is firm.

4 Turn the vanilla gelato into a large bowl and let stand at room temperature for 10 to 15 minutes. Drain the fruits and add them to the gelato along with the chocolate chips. Fold and stir to incorporate them as evenly as possible. Pack into the loaf pan, cover again, and freeze for at least 2 hours.

5 Soften the chocolate gelato by letting it stand at room temperature for 10 to 15 minutes. Spread it on top to fill the loaf pan. Cover with any remaining slices of pound cake. Cover and freeze for at least 1 hour and up to 2 days. To serve, invert the cassata to unmold onto a platter. Peel off the plastic. Let the loaf stand in the refrigerator for 5 to 10 minutes. Cut into thick slices and serve on chilled dessert plates with a drizzle of chocolate sauce on top.

INGREDIENTS

¼ cup mixed glacé (candied) fruits

3 tablespoons dark rum or brandy

2 all-butter pound cakes (10¾ ounces or 284 grams each), thawed if frozen

1 pint (450 ml) Pistachio Gelato (page 13), or your favorite premium brand ice cream or gelato

1 pint (450 ml) vanilla gelato or ice cream

¼ cup mini chocolate chips

1 pint (450 ml) chocolate gelato or ice cream

Easy Chocolate Sauce (page 184)

Serves 8

Italian Tartufo

These chocolate-coated ice cream treats are named for the black truffles they resemble. While they are often coated in crisp chocolate, at home it's easier to roll them in grated chocolate or sweetened cocoa powder.

1 In a small jar, combine the cherries and brandy. Cover and let stand at room temperature, shaking occasionally, for at least 2 hours or as long as 24 hours. Line 8 (6-ounce or 175-gram) custard cups or 8 (2½-inch or 6¼-cm) muffin tins with 8-inch (20-cm) squares of plastic wrap. (Later you will need this excess to completely enclose the filling.)

2 Soften the chocolate ice cream at room temperature for 10 to 15 minutes. Spread it over the bottom and about two-thirds up the sides of the lined cups, leaving a deep well in the center. Reserve about one-third of the ice cream to cover the tops of the cups later; return to the freezer until needed. Freeze the cups, covered, until the ice cream is firm to the touch, at least 1 hour.

3 Soften the hazelnut ice cream at room temperature for 10 to 15 minutes. Drain the cherries, reserving the brandy for another use. Fill the cavity in each cup with the hazelnut ice cream, then press a cherry into the center of each. Freeze, covered, until firm to the touch, about 30 minutes.

4 Soften the remaining chocolate ice cream at room temperature for 5 to 10 minutes. Pack onto the tops of the molds to cover completely. Cover and freeze until firm, at least 1 hour.

5 Use the ends of the plastic wrap to lift the ice cream from the cup. Form the plastic-covered ice cream into balls. Twist the ends of the wrap to seal. Freeze until firm, at least 4 hours. To serve, unwrap the tartufo and roll in the grated chocolate to coat.

INGREDIENTS

8   maraschino cherries, stems removed, well drained

¼   cup brandy or dark rum

1   pint (450 ml) Chocolate Custard Ice Cream (page 30), or your favorite premium brand ice cream or gelato

1   pint (450 ml) hazelnut ice cream or gelato, or any other flavor, such as coffee or cherry-vanilla

2   ounces (about ¼ cup) finely grated semisweet chocolate, or ¼ cup sweet ground chocolate and cocoa (such as Ghirardelli® brand), or other sweetened cocoa powder

Serves 8

Hidden Treasure
Ice Cream Cupcakes

Kids of all ages love the combination of cake and ice cream, and here the concept is made even more appealing with individual servings formed into ice cream cupcakes. The easy, egg-free batter bakes into a moist crumb, and the dessert can be made a week in advance and frozen.

1 Preheat the oven to 350°F (180°C). Line a 12-cup muffin tin with paper liners and set aside. In a large bowl, combine the flour, sugar, cocoa powder, baking soda, and salt. Whisk to blend.

2 In another bowl, combine the water, oil, vinegar, and vanilla. Add to the dry ingredients, beating with an electric mixer until smooth.

3 Pour the batter into the muffin tins, filling each cup until approximately two-thirds full. Tap the pan on the counter to remove any air bubbles.

4 Bake for 25 minutes, or until a tester inserted in the center of a cupcake comes out with moist crumbs clinging to it. Let the cupcakes cool in the pan for 5 minutes, then transfer them in their paper liners to a wire rack to cool completely.

5 With a serrated knife, cut the top third off of each cupcake and set aside. Using a melon baller or a serrated grapefruit knife, cut out the center of the cupcake bottoms, leaving a ½-inch (1¼-cm) shell all around and at the bottom. Place a small scoop of ice cream in the cupcake shell and replace the top; don't worry if some of the ice cream shows. If made in advance, wrap individually and freeze.

6 If serving with fudge sauce, peel off and discard the paper liners. Pour 2 tablespoons of fudge sauce on each dessert plate. Place the cupcake on top and serve with a fork.

INGREDIENTS

1½ cups all-purpose flour

1   cup sugar

⅓   cup Dutch process unsweetened cocoa powder

1   teaspoon baking soda

½   teaspoon salt

1   cup cold water

⅓   cup vegetable oil

1   tablespoon distilled white vinegar

1½ teaspoons vanilla extract

1   pint (450 ml) White Chocolate Ice Cream (page 26) or your favorite homemade or store-bought flavor

Haute Fudge Sauce (optional; page 116)

Makes 12

COOL TIPS FOR SUCCESS

Serving frozen desserts on chilled plates will slow the melting process.

Watermelon Bombe

Here is a dessert that will bring a smile to everybody's face. What looks like a thick slice of watermelon is really an ice cream and sorbet surprise studded with chocolate chips.

INGREDIENTS

1½ pints (675 ml) Tahitian Double Vanilla Ice Cream (page 12), or your favorite vanilla ice cream, softened slightly

3 tablespoons mini chocolate chips

1½ pints (675 ml) Watermelon-Raspberry Sorbet (page 96), or other pink or red sorbet, softened slightly

Green food coloring

Serves 6 to 8

1 Lightly spray the inside of a 6-cup melon-shaped mold (about 9 inches or 23 cm long) with nonstick cooking spray; freeze for at least 30 minutes. (Alternatively, line the inside of a 6-cup freezer-safe bowl with 2 crisscrossed sheets of plastic wrap, letting the plastic hang over the sides.) Refrigerate until needed.

2 Using a rubber spatula or a large spoon, spread the vanilla ice cream in the bottom and up the sides of the chilled mold, creating a cavity in the center for the sorbet. Cover with plastic wrap, pressing against the ice cream to seal tightly and press out any air pockets. Freeze for 4 hours, or until very firm.

3 Fold the chocolate chips into the softened sorbet. Pack the studded sorbet into the cavity of the vanilla ice cream, pressing down to remove any air pockets. Cover again with plastic wrap and freeze for 2 hours, or until firm.

4 Dip the mold into very hot water for 6 seconds to loosen. Remove the plastic wrap and invert onto a chilled serving platter. Freeze until the ice cream is firm to the touch, about 15 minutes.

5 Use a few drops of undiluted food coloring to paint the outside of the molded ice cream with a pastry brush. Do not try for uniform color; variegated stripes are more realistic. Freeze for 15 minutes, or until the ice cream is firm to the touch. Cover tightly with plastic wrap and freeze until very hard, at least 2 hours, or up to 3 days. Cut into thick slices with a long, sharp knife dipped in hot water and wiped dry. Serve at once on chilled dessert plates.

Ice Cream Spaghetti

In Italy, this is actually an adult dessert, but how much nicer for children: an ice-cold plate of frozen "spaghetti," complete with red sauce and cheese—even meatballs and garlic bread, if you like. To get the right effect, you'll need an old-fashioned potato ricer or spaetzle maker.

1 Place the potato ricer and a large platter in the freezer to chill for 15 minutes. In a small bowl, beat the jelly with a fork until it is soft and fluid.

2 Using a large serrated knife, cut crosswise through the ice cream carton to divide the ice cream in half. Peel away the carton and pack the cold ice cream into the potato ricer. Use firm, steady pressure to push the ice cream slowly through the ricer, moving your hands in a circular motion to mimic the look of a plate of spaghetti. Repeat with the remaining ice cream.

3 Working quickly, drizzle with the jelly. You can use the large holes on a box grater to grate white chocolate over the top to resemble Parmesan cheese. Return the platter to the freezer for 15 minutes, or until firm to the touch. Serve at once, or cover with plastic wrap and freeze for up to 2 days. Let stand for 5 to 10 minutes in the refrigerator to soften slightly. Garnish with the "meatballs" and "garlic bread" just before serving.

INGREDIENTS

½ cup strawberry jelly or thick strawberry sauce

1 pint (450 ml) French vanilla ice cream, softened slightly but still firm enough to hold its shape

2 ounces (50 grams) white chocolate, at room temperature (optional)

Optional garnishes:

For meatballs, use small chocolate truffles, rolled in cocoa powder or finely chopped nuts.

For garlic bread, toast slices of pound cake and trim to resemble garlic bread. Top with a few tablespoons of apricot jam mixed with 1 teaspoon minced fresh mint to simulate garlic butter.

Serves 2

Frozen Bonbons

Sometimes after a big meal, you want just a bite of something sweet. Here's a portion-controlled dessert that's perfect with after-dinner coffee or as a bite-size snack in the late afternoon: miniature ice cream bonbons, coated with dark chocolate and frozen solid.

1 Stack 2 baking sheets lined with waxed paper and place in the freezer until cold, about 15 minutes. Using a small (1-inch or 2½-cm) ice cream scoop, a large melon baller, or a tablespoon, scoop out small balls of ice cream about 1 inch (2½-cm) in diameter and set them on one of the sheets. Working quickly, insert a toothpick into the center of each ice cream ball. Freeze for 3 hours, or until hard.

2 Place a small heatproof bowl over a pot of barely simmering water. Add the chocolate and cook over very low heat, stirring, until melted and smooth. Remove from the heat, add the coconut oil or butter and the salt, and stir until smooth.

3 Remove the ice cream balls from the freezer. Working quickly, one at a time, lift an ice cream ball by the toothpick and hold it over the bowl of melted chocolate. Ladle the melted chocolate over the ice cream ball, turning the ball to coat it completely, and letting the excess chocolate run back into the bowl. Place each finished ball on the second sheet in the freezer. Repeat with the remaining ice cream balls. Freeze for 4 hours, or until very firm. Remove the toothpicks. Serve at once, or cover with plastic wrap and transfer to a freezer-safe container to store for up to 1 week.

INGREDIENTS

1 pint (450 ml) your favorite flavor ice cream, gelato, or frozen custard

7 ounces (200 grams) bittersweet chocolate

2 tablespoons coconut oil or melted unsalted butter

Dash of salt

Makes about 2 dozen

Fruited Marsala Chestnut Bombes

While the flavor used to be associated with a lot of labor, these days, fully cooked and peeled chestnuts are available in jars and vacuum-sealed packages in many supermarkets and club stores. *Crème de marrons* is sweetened chestnut puree, usually packaged in small tins or tubes. It comes plain or flavored with vanilla. Either is fine for this recipe.

1 In a small bowl, combine the chopped chestnuts, currants, orange peel, candied cherries, and Marsala. Cover and let stand at room temperature overnight. Drain the fruits, reserving the liquid.

2 Line 4 (6-ounce or 175-gram) custard cups or molds with enough plastic wrap to drape generously over the sides.

3 Turn the ice cream into a large bowl and let stand at room temperature for about 10 minutes to soften slightly. Drop spoonfuls of the chopped chestnuts and fruits and ½ cup of the chestnut puree over the ice cream. Using a stiff plastic spatula or a blunt knife, gently cut and fold to marble the ingredients into the ice cream. Don't worry if some larger pockets remain.

4 Pack the marbled ice cream into the lined molds and cover each with plastic wrap. Freeze until firm, at least 6 hours or overnight.

5 To make the sauce, mix together the remaining ¼ cup chestnut puree with the reserved Marsala. Remove each ice cream from its mold and invert onto a dessert plate; peel off the plastic wrap. Drizzle about 2 tablespoons of the sauce over each dessert and top with whipped cream.

INGREDIENTS

½ cup finely chopped, peeled, cooked chestnuts

1 tablespoon currants or raisins

1 tablespoon chopped candied orange peel

1 tablespoon chopped candied red cherries

⅓ cup sweet Marsala

1 pint (450 ml) Tahitian Double Vanilla Ice Cream (page 12), or your favorite premium brand

¾ cup chestnut puree (crème de marrons)

Whipped cream, for garnish

Serves 4

Warm Chocolate-Espresso Tart with Espresso Gelato

This decidedly adult combo contrasts a warm, intensely chocolate tart with a scoop of cold espresso-flavored ice cream on the side. If you are lucky enough to have any of the tart left over the next day, it is also good served at room temperature or cold.

1 Preheat the oven to 375°F (190°C). In a medium saucepan, combine the cream, milk, espresso powder, and salt. Cook over medium heat, stirring frequently, just until bubbles appear around the edges of the pan. Remove from the heat.

2 Add the chocolate to the hot espresso cream and stir until melted and smooth. Set aside and let cool to lukewarm, about 20 minutes. Whisk in the egg until thoroughly blended.

3 Place the prepared pastry shell on a baking sheet. Pour the chocolate filling into the shell. Bake for 12 to 15 minutes, or until the filling is almost firm but still trembling in the center. Transfer to a wire rack and let cool for about 30 minutes.

4 To serve, remove the fluted rim from the tart pan. Cut the warm tart into wedges and transfer to individual dessert plates. Serve with a large scoop of Espresso Bean Gelato on the side. Dust with cocoa powder and serve at once.

INGREDIENTS

¾ cup heavy cream

⅓ cup whole milk

2 teaspoons instant espresso powder

Dash of salt

7 ounces (200 grams) semisweet chocolate, finely chopped

1 egg, lightly beaten

Shortbread Pastry Shell, baked and cooled (page 186)

1 quart (1 liter) Espresso Bean Gelato (page 37), or store-bought coffee ice cream

Dutch process unsweetened cocoa powder, for dusting

Serves 8 to 10

erry Shortcakes with
late-Buttermilk Biscuits

How can you improve upon a traditional strawberry shortcake? Add ice cream and chocolate, of course!

1 In a large bowl, combine the berries, sugar, and lemon juice. Stir to mix, coarsely mashing about ¼ of the berries with a fork. Let stand for 15 minutes to dissolve the sugar.

2 To assemble, use a serrated knife to carefully split each biscuit in half horizontally. Place the bottom halves cut-sides up on 4 dessert plates. Top each with a large spoonful of berries and their juice and a scoop of ice cream. Cover with the biscuit tops. Dollop whipped cream over the shortcakes and top with the remaining berries. Garnish with Chocolate Curls and serve at once.

Chocolate-Buttermilk Biscuits

1 Preheat the oven to 425°F (220°C). In a food processor, combine the flour, cocoa powder, sugar, baking powder, baking soda, and salt. Process briefly to blend. Add the butter and pulse until the dough resembles coarse meal. With the machine on, slowly pour in the buttermilk. Add the chocolate chips and pulse 2 or 3 times.

2 Scrape the dough onto a lightly floured work surface. Knead 2 or 3 times until smooth. Roll or pat the dough into an even 1-inch (2½-cm) thickness. Using a 3-inch (7½-cm) biscuit cutter dipped in flour, cut out 4 biscuits. If needed, gather together the dough trimmings, pat them out again, and cut out more biscuits.

3 Arrange the biscuits 2 inches (5 cm) apart on a parchment-lined or lightly greased baking sheet. Use a dry pastry brush to remove excess flour from the tops of the biscuits. Bake for 12 to 14 minutes, or until the tops appear dry and spring back when touched lightly. Transfer the biscuits to a wire rack to cool.

INGREDIENTS

4 cups fresh berries (any combination of sliced strawberries or whole blueberries, raspberries, or blackberries)

1½ tablespoons sugar

1 teaspoon fresh lemon juice

1 pint (450 ml) Almost-Instant Strawberry Ice Cream (page 20), or store-bought berry or vanilla ice cream

4 Chocolate-Buttermilk Biscuits (recipe follows)

Whipped cream, for garnish

Chocolate Curls (page 187), for garnish

Serves 4

Chocolate-Buttermilk Biscuits

1 cup all-purpose flour

¼ cup Dutch process unsweetened cocoa powder

¼ cup sugar

1 teaspoon baking powder

½ teaspoon baking soda

¼ teaspoon salt

4 tablespoons cold unsalted butter, cut into 8 pieces

6 tablespoons buttermilk

⅓ cup chocolate chips

Makes 4

Chocolate Ice Cream Sandwiches

These easy rolled chocolate cookies are the perfect texture for ice cream sandwiches: tender and not overly brittle.

1 In a medium bowl, combine the flour, cocoa powder, and salt. Whisk gently to blend the dry ingredients.

2 In a large bowl with an electric mixer, beat the butter for 1 minute. Gradually beat in the sugar until light and fluffy. Add the egg and vanilla and beat well. Gradually beat in the dry ingredients until well blended. Cover and refrigerate for 2 hours, or until firm.

3 Preheat the oven to 350°F (180°C). On a lightly floured surface, roll out the cookie dough to a thickness of about ⅜ inch (1 cm). You don't want these too thin. Cut out cookies with a 2½-inch (6¼-cm) round cutter and carefully transfer them to 1 or 2 parchment-lined or lightly greased cookie sheets, spacing the cookies at least 1 inch (2½ cm) apart. Gather any scraps into a ball and roll out to make more cookies.

4 Bake for 10 to 12 minutes, or until the bottoms are set. The tops will still be slightly soft; do not overbake. Transfer the cookies to a wire rack and let cool completely.

5 Arrange 12 cookies flat-side up on a baking sheet. Using a 2-inch (5-cm) ice cream scoop (#24) or a large spoon, place about ¼ cup of ice cream on each cookie. Cover with the remaining cookies, pressing down gently to form a sandwich. Smooth the edges, if desired. Working quickly, roll the sandwiches in the chocolate sprinkles or chopped nuts to coat the edges. Freeze uncovered until firm to the touch, about 30 minutes.

6 Wrap the sandwiches individually in squares of plastic wrap. Place in an airtight container and freeze for at least 2 hours, or until firm.

INGREDIENTS

1½ cups all-purpose flour

¾ cup Dutch process unsweetened cocoa powder

⅛ teaspoon salt

1½ sticks (6 ounces or 175 grams) unsalted butter, at room temperature

1 cup sugar

1 egg

½ teaspoon vanilla extract

3 cups Tahitian Double Vanilla Ice Cream (page 12), or your favorite premium brand

½ cup chocolate sprinkles (jimmies) or finely chopped roasted peanuts or other nuts

Makes about 2 dozen (2½-inch or 6¼-cm) cookies, to make 12 sandwiches

Chocolate Chip Birthday "Pizza" with Scoops du Jour

Three of kids' favorite foods all bound up in one: a chocolate chip ice cream pizza. If you prefer to serve the pizza directly from the pan, omit the parchment and simply grease and flour the baking sheet instead.

1 Preheat the oven to 375°F (190°C). Line a pizza pan or large cookie sheet with a 14-inch (35-cm) round of parchment paper. In a medium bowl, combine the flour, baking soda, and salt; set the dry ingredients aside.

2 In a large bowl, combine the butter, brown sugar, granulated sugar, and vanilla. Beat with an electric mixer until light and creamy. Beat in the egg until well blended. With the mixer on low, gradually add the dry ingredients. Mix in the chocolate chips by hand until just blended. Scrape the dough onto the parchment and pat into an even layer 12 inches (30 cm) in diameter.

3 Bake for 20 to 25 minutes, or until the center is set; the edges need not be browned. Transfer the pan to a wire rack and let cool completely. Carefully slide the cookie "pizza" onto a large serving platter, using the ends of the parchment to help pull; otherwise, leave on the pan. Cover tightly with plastic wrap and freeze until cold, at least 30 minutes or up to 4 days.

4 Spread an even layer of softened vanilla ice cream over the top. Cover and freeze for 30 minutes. Then, working quickly and using a small (1½-inch or 3¾-cm) ice cream scoop, dollop round balls of chocolate and strawberry ice cream all over the cookie crust. Decorate with colored sprinkles and Chocolate Curls and freeze uncovered until firm; then wrap in plastic wrap.

5 About 30 minutes before serving, unwrap the "pizza" and let soften in the refrigerator for 15 to 20 minutes before cutting.

INGREDIENTS

2¼ cups all-purpose flour

1 teaspoon baking soda

½ teaspoon salt

2 sticks (8 ounces or 225 grams) unsalted butter, at room temperature

1 cup (packed) dark brown sugar

¼ cup granulated sugar

2 teaspoons vanilla extract

1 egg

2 cups (12 ounces or 350 grams) semisweet chocolate chips

1 pint (450 ml) Tahitian Double Vanilla Ice Cream (page 12), or your favorite premium brand, softened slightly

1 pint (450 ml) Chocolate Custard Ice Cream (page 30), or your favorite premium brand

1 pint (450 ml) Almost-Instant Strawberry Ice Cream (page 20), or your favorite premium brand

Colored sprinkles (jimmies) and Chocolate Curls (page 187), for garnish

Serves 10 to 12

Frozen Chocolate Pudding Pops

Boiled pudding is unbelievably easy. This one is eggless, so there is no worry of curdling—and it's ready for the freezer in 15 minutes or less.

1 In a medium saucepan, combine the sugar, cocoa, cornstarch, and salt. Whisk gently to blend. Place over medium heat and gradually whisk in the milk. Bring to a boil, whisking until thickened and smooth, 5 to 7 minutes. Remove from the heat and add the chocolate chips; stir until melted and smooth. Stir in the vanilla and set aside for 5 minutes to cool slightly.

2 Divide the pudding among 8 (4- to 5-ounce or 100- to 150-gram) plastic pop molds or paper cups and freeze for 1 hour, or until partially frozen. Follow the package directions for inserting the plastic sticks provided, or insert a wooden frozen dessert stick or sturdy plastic spoon into the center of each cup. Freeze for 4 hours, or until very firm.

3 Unmold as the package directs; or, if using cups, tear off the paper. Serve at once, or cover with plastic wrap and store in the freezer for up to 3 days.

INGREDIENTS

⅔ cup sugar

¼ cup Dutch process unsweetened cocoa powder

¼ cup cornstarch

¼ teaspoon salt

3 cups milk

½ cup semisweet chocolate chips

½ teaspoon vanilla extract

Makes 8 pops

Fruit Smoothie Pops

Keep a batch of these healthy snacks in the freezer, and kids can help themselves anytime they like. Appropriate blunt wooden sticks or plastic handles are sold in craft stores and in some supermarket produce sections.

1 In a blender, combine the fruit, milk, yogurt, and honey. Process for 30 seconds, or until thick and smooth.

2 Pour into 8 (4- to 5-ounce or 100- to 150-gram) plastic pop molds or paper cups and freeze for 1 hour, or until partially frozen. Follow the package directions for inserting the plastic sticks provided, or insert a wooden frozen dessert stick or sturdy plastic spoon into the center of each cup. Freeze for 3 hours, or until very firm.

3 Unmold the pops as the package directs. If using cups, tear off the paper. Serve at once, or cover with plastic wrap and store in the freezer for up to 3 days.

INGREDIENTS

2 cups assorted fruits, such as bananas, strawberries, raspberries, and peaches

1½ cups milk

1 cup plain yogurt

⅓ cup honey or maple syrup

Makes about 8 pops

"we dare not trust our wit
for making our house pleasant to
our friends, so we buy
ice cream."

–writer Ralph Waldo Emerson

almost–instant frozen desserts

Chocolate Cookie
Ice Cream Cake

Here's an almost-instant cake the kids will love. As long as the cake is tightly wrapped, it can be made weeks in advance and frozen, so it's all ready to be pulled out whenever you need a dessert everyone will love.

1 Preheat the oven to 375°F (190°C). Spread out the almonds on a baking sheet and toast them in the oven until lightly browned and fragrant, 10 to 12 minutes. Transfer to a plate and let cool.

2 Break up the cookies roughly into quarters. In 2 batches, combine the toasted almonds and chocolate cookies in a food processor and pulse to chop very coarsely. Transfer to a bowl and mix in the chocolate chips.

3 Line the bottom of a round 8- or 9-inch (20- or 23-cm) springform pan with waxed paper, parchment, or foil. Open the ice cream and use a large knife to cut into ¾- to 1-inch (2- to 2½-cm) slices. As you cut each slice, fit it flat against the bottom of the pan. When most of the bottom is covered, smooth with a plastic spatula or metal spoon to fill in any gaps. Sprinkle one-third of the chocolate-almond crumbs over the ice cream to make an even layer. Cover with another layer of ice cream and another layer of the chocolate-almond crumbs. Repeat the layers until all the ice cream and crumbs have been used. Double wrap in plastic and freeze.

4 A couple of hours before serving, remove the cake from the freezer and unwrap. Using a blunt knife dipped in hot water and wiped dry, cut around the sides of the pan to separate the ice cream from the metal. Remove the sides of the pan. Smooth the sides of the cake with a rubber spatula and place in the freezer for 5 to 10 minutes to firm up; then re-wrap the cake and return to the freezer until serving time.

INGREDIENTS

½ cup natural almonds (about 2 ounces or 50 grams)

½ of a (9-ounce or 250-gram) box of chocolate wafer cookies

¾ cup mini chocolate chips

½ gallon carton of French vanilla ice cream

Serves 8 to 10

Frozen Cannoli

These are instant in the sense that you don't have to make anything, but the assembled cannoli must be filled in advance so that they have time to set fully in the freezer. Choose a sauce that complements the flavor of ice cream you've chosen, and if using the chocolate or caramel sauce, heat gently before serving.

1   Let the ice cream stand at room temperature for 10 to 15 minutes to soften slightly. Fit a large pastry bag with a large plain tip or use a large heavy-duty zippered plastic bag and cut off one of the bottom corners. Fill with the ice cream.

2   Working quickly with one cannoli at a time, insert the tip of the pastry bag into the shell and fill with ice cream. Place the filled cannoli on a baking sheet and place in the freezer for at least 2 hours or overnight.

3   Remove the ice cream–filled cannoli from the freezer 10 to 15 minutes before serving. Meanwhile, warm the sauce over low heat, if needed. Place each cannoli on a dessert plate and drizzle with the sauce of your choice. Sprinkle the cannoli with nuts and serve at once.

INGREDIENTS

1½ pints (675 ml) ice cream, your choice of flavor

12   cannoli shells

1   cup Easy Chocolate Sauce (page 184), Caramel Sauce (page 185), or Raspberry Sauce (page 66)

Chopped toasted almonds, walnuts, or pistachios, for garnish

Serves 6

Rainbow Ice Cream and Sorbet Torte

This super-easy, sophisticated-looking frozen torte draws its inspiration from the classic children's treat, layering the fruit sorbet and vanilla ice cream that usually comes paired on a stick. Top with a few fresh raspberries and a sprig of mint, or a drizzle of Raspberry Sauce (page 66), if you like.

1 Let the orange sherbet soften enough so you can scoop it out easily. Pack into the bottom of a 9-inch (23-cm) springform pan. Cover with plastic wrap and freeze for 30 to 60 minutes, or until the sherbet hardens.

2 Let 1 pint (450 ml) of the ice cream soften slightly. Pack that over the sherbet. Cover and return to the freezer until set.

3 Let the Watermelon-Raspberry Sorbet soften slightly. Pack that over the ice cream.

4 Soften the second pint of ice cream and pack that over the Watermelon-Raspberry Sorbet. Cover and freeze for at least 2 hours, or overnight.

5 To serve, dip a blunt knife in a glass of hot water, quickly wipe it dry, and run the warm knife around the edge of the springform. Remove the sides of the pan. Supporting the torte on the metal bottom, rotate the dessert while pressing the chopped pistachios into the side to coat completely.

6 Set the torte on a warm, damp towel for about 10 seconds to loosen the bottom. Invert onto a large round platter and carefully remove the metal bottom of the pan. If necessary, smooth the top of the torte with a warm spatula. Cut into wedges to serve.

INGREDIENTS

1 pint (450 ml) Orange Sherbet (page 49), or store-bought orange sorbet

2 pints (900 ml) French vanilla ice cream

1 pint (450 ml) Watermelon-Raspberry Sorbet (page 96), or store-bought raspberry sorbet

1 cup chopped pistachio nuts (about 3 ounces or 75 grams)

Serves 10 to 12

Mile-High Lemon Chiffon Ice Cream Pie

Lofty enough to make an impression, this airy ice cream pie also has an exaggerated lemon flavor. It's one dessert you can make well ahead of time, because the texture actually improves after several days in the freezer. Lemon curd is usually found in the jams and jellies section of the supermarket.

1   In a large bowl, beat the egg whites and salt until the whites stand in soft, foamy peaks. Continue to beat as you gradually add the sugar in a thin, steady stream. Beat until the whites stand in stiff, firm peaks.

2   In a small bowl, whisk together the lemon curd, lemon zest, and lemon juice. Using a large rubber spatula, carefully fold the lemon curd mixture into the beaten egg whites until evenly incorporated without deflating the whites.

3   Place the ice cream in a large bowl and mash with a rubber spatula to make it malleable but not melted. Working quickly, scoop the egg whites over the ice cream and fold until the mixture is almost blended; it's okay if there are a few white streaks. Pile into the prepared crust, mounding it in the center, and immediately place the pie in the freezer. Freeze for at least 6 hours.

4   If you are not serving the pie the same day, carefully cover it with plastic wrap and freeze for up to 4 days. To serve, let the pie sit in the refrigerator for 15 minutes before slicing into wedges with a long, sharp knife dipped in hot water and wiped dry.

INGREDIENTS

4   egg whites

Dash of salt

⅓   cup sugar

¾   cup lemon curd

1   tablespoon grated lemon zest

2   tablespoons fresh lemon juice

1½ quarts (1½ liters) vanilla ice cream, softened slightly

Gingersnap Crumb Crust (page 186), or a 9-inch (23-cm) prepared graham cracker crust, baked and chilled

Serves 6 to 8

COOL TIPS FOR SUCCESS

Frozen pies and other desserts benefit from softening in the refrigerator for 10 minutes (or as the recipe directs) before serving. The ice cream should still be firm but just manageable enough to scoop or slice. Remember that once cut, individual servings of homemade ice cream will soften quickly.

Island Frozen Yogurt Pie with Banana-Rum Sauce

Frozen yogurt nestled in a crunchy cereal crust sounds innocent enough . . . until it is bathed in a decadent Caramel Banana-Rum Sauce. Weetabix®, an organic, whole-grain cereal imported from Canada and the United Kingdom, can be found on many American food market shelves. If you are unable to locate it, substitute 16 (2-inch or 5-cm) graham crackers.

1 Preheat the oven to 375°F (190°C). Lightly coat a 9-inch (23-cm) pie plate with nonstick cooking spray. In a large bowl, crush the cereal with your fingers until it is broken into crumbs.

2 Melt the butter in a small saucepan over low heat, or in the microwave in a microwave-safe container. Add the sugar, stirring until it is dissolved. Add to the crushed cereal, stirring to coat. Press the mixture onto the bottom and up the sides of the prepared pie plate. Bake 10 to 12 minutes, or until the crust is set and lightly browned at the edges. Transfer to a wire rack to cool completely.

3 Soften the frozen yogurt by letting it stand at room temperature for 10 minutes. Pack the yogurt into the cool shell, pressing down lightly to remove any air pockets. Cover the surface of the yogurt with plastic wrap and freeze until firm, at least 4 hours or overnight.

4 To serve, let the pie soften for 15 minutes in the refrigerator before cutting into wedges with a long, sharp knife dipped in hot water and wiped dry. Top each serving with a drizzle of Caramel Banana-Rum Sauce.

INGREDIENTS

5	Weetabix® biscuits
⅓	cup unsalted butter
2	tablespoons light or dark brown sugar
1	quart (1 liter) vanilla or dulce de leche frozen yogurt

Caramel Banana-Rum Sauce (page 185)

Serves 8

Chocolate–Peanut Butter Pie

There are certain kinds of people who cannot get enough of chocolate and peanut butter. This frozen pie is dedicated to them, as well as to those who love them. It is a sweet dessert, so portion accordingly.

1 Prepare and bake the crust as directed. Let cool, then place in the freezer to chill thoroughly.

2 In a large bowl, combine the softened vanilla and chocolate ice cream, the peanuts, and the marshmallows. Using a large wooden spoon or stiff plastic spatula, stir and mash them together, working until the ice creams are marbled with prominent streaks of chocolate and vanilla. Drop heaping spoonfuls of both the peanut butter and chocolate sauce over the mixture. Working quickly, stir and mash them into the ice cream, blending only partially, so you also see streaks of peanut butter and chocolate in the ice cream.

3 Pile the mixture into the prepared crust, mounding it in the center. Freeze for at least 6 hours before serving. If you are not serving the pie the same day, carefully cover it with plastic wrap and freeze for up to 3 days.

4 To serve, let the pie stand in the refrigerator for 15 minutes before slicing into wedges with a long, sharp knife dipped in hot water and wiped dry.

INGREDIENTS

Chocolate Crumb Crust (page 187), or a 9-inch (23-cm) prepared chocolate cookie crust

3 cups vanilla ice cream, softened slightly

3 cups chocolate ice cream, softened slightly

½ cup coarsely chopped roasted peanuts (salted or unsalted)

1 cup miniature marshmallows

1 cup smooth peanut butter, chilled

⅔ cup chocolate or fudge sauce or topping (not chocolate syrup), homemade or store-bought, chilled

Serves 6 to 8

Adobe Pie

In Mississippi, people say their chocolate-crusted ice cream pie drenched in fudge sauce is made from "mud." Southwesterners refer to their version as "adobe." Whatever you call it, this sumptuous dessert is perfect for casual entertaining, because you can make it several days in advance and hold it in the freezer. Save time, if you wish, by using a store-bought chocolate cookie crust.

1 Prepare the Chocolate Crumb Crust as directed and chill thoroughly.

2 Pour about ½ cup of the Mocha Fudge Sauce into the crust and freeze for 30 minutes, or until firm.

3 Working quickly, use a rubber spatula to spread the vanilla ice cream over the fudge sauce, mounding it slightly in the center. Cover with plastic wrap and freeze for 1 hour, or until firm.

4 Spread the coffee ice cream in an even layer over the vanilla, again mounding it slightly in the center. Sprinkle Chocolate Curls all over the top of the pie. Freeze for 1 hour. Carefully cover with plastic wrap and freeze for at least 5 more hours or up to 4 days.

5 To serve, let the pie sit in the refrigerator for about 15 minutes to soften just slightly before slicing into wedges with a long, sharp knife dipped in hot water and wiped dry. Drizzle a couple of tablespoons of Mocha Fudge Sauce alongside — not over — each slice.

INGREDIENTS

Chocolate Crumb Crust (page 187), or a 9-inch (23-cm) prepared chocolate cookie crust

Mocha Fudge Sauce (page 184), or your favorite chocolate sauce

3 cups vanilla ice cream, softened slightly

3 cups coffee ice cream, softened slightly

Chocolate Curls (page 187) or 2 ounces (50 grams) semisweet chocolate, coarsely grated

Serves 6 to 8

Mocha Madness
Ice Cream Pie

One taste of this easy-to-make pie, and you'll understand why it is so popular. The chocolate cereal "crust" ends up tasting like a candy bar. If you like, vary the ice cream flavor to suit your mood, or try using butterscotch, peanut butter, or mint-flavored chips instead of semisweet chocolate.

1 Press a 12-inch (30-cm) sheet of aluminum foil into the bottom and up the sides of a 9-inch (23-cm) pie pan, letting the excess drape over the edge. Spray with nonstick cooking spray.

2 Place a large heatproof bowl over a pot of barely simmering water. Add the chocolate and butter and cook over low heat, stirring, until melted and smooth. Add the cereal, stirring to coat well. Using the back of a spoon, form a shell by pressing the warm mixture into the bottom and up the sides of the foil in the prepared pie pan. Freeze for 30 minutes, or until the shell is very cold and firm. Use the edges of the foil to remove the crisped rice shell from the pan. Carefully peel off and discard the foil; return the shell to the pan.

3 Soften the ice cream by letting it stand at room temperature for 10 minutes. Pack the ice cream into the cold shell, pressing down lightly to remove any air pockets. Cover and freeze until the ice cream is very firm, at least 4 hours or up to 3 days.

4 To serve, let the pie soften for 15 minutes in the refrigerator. Spoon or pipe the whipped cream over the top of the pie. Garnish with chocolate-covered espresso beans and chocolate shavings. Cut into wedges with a long, sharp knife dipped in hot water and wiped dry. Serve warm, with Mocha Fudge Sauce on the side.

INGREDIENTS

½ cup (3 ounces or 75 grams) semisweet chocolate chips

2 tablespoons unsalted butter, cut into pieces

2 cups crisped rice cereal (such as Kellogg's Rice Krispies®)

1 quart (1 liter) coffee ice cream

1 cup heavy cream, whipped

Chocolate-covered espresso beans and chocolate shavings, for garnish

Mocha Fudge Sauce (page 184)

Serves 8

Ice Cream Fairy Cakes

This combines everything kids love at a birthday party: chocolate chip cookies, ice cream, candy sprinkles, individual portions, and no plates or utensils! These can be completely assembled and frozen weeks in advance if you use non-dairy whipped topping instead of whipped cream. But if you wait and allow the children to squirt canned whipped cream onto their own fairy cakes, they will surely deem your party the social event of the season.

1 Preheat the oven to 350°F (180°C). Line 2 standard 12-cup cupcake pans with paper liners, or arrange 24 foil baking cups 1 inch (2½ cm) apart on a baking sheet.

2 Break or cut the cookie dough along the pre-scored surface to make 24 squares of dough. Place 1 piece of dough in each baking cup.

3 Bake for 10 to 12 minutes, or until the cookies are barely set. They will firm up as they cool. Let cool completely in the pans.

4 Place 1 small scoop of ice cream on top of each cookie. Press down gently with the back of a spoon to remove any air pockets. If using non-dairy whipped topping, spread over the ice cream at this point. Cover the pans with plastic wrap and freeze for at least 4 hours or as long as 1 week. Once the fairy cakes are frozen, they can be removed from the metal pans and stored in an airtight container.

5 If using canned whipped cream, squirt it on just before serving. Garnish with the candy sprinkles.

INGREDIENTS

1 package (18 ounces or 500 grams) refrigerated pre-scored chocolate chip cookie dough (such as Nestlé brand)

2 quarts (2 liters) of your child's favorite flavor ice cream

1 tub (8 ounces or 225 grams) frozen non-dairy whipped topping, thawed, or 1 can (14 ounces or 400 grams) Reddi-wip®

Colored or chocolate sprinkles (jimmies), for garnish

Makes 24

Phony Spumoni

Italian spumoni is gelato, often a couple of flavors, usually lightened with whipped cream and blended with candied fruit and nuts. This simplified version mixes vanilla ice cream with toasted almonds, pistachio nuts, maraschino cherries, candied orange peel, and bittersweet chocolate to simulate the more sophisticated dessert.

1 Preheat the oven to 325°F (160°C). Line an 8-inch (20-cm) round cake pan with plastic wrap, leaving enough extra to extend over the rim of the pan.

2 Spread out the almond slices in a small baking pan and toast in the oven until lightly browned and fragrant, 5 to 7 minutes. Transfer to a plate and let cool. Coarsely chop 2 tablespoons of the almonds.

3 Let the ice cream stand at room temperature for 10 to 15 minutes so that it is just malleable. Quickly stir in the chopped toasted almonds, pistachio nuts, chocolate, chopped cherries with the reserved juice, and candied orange peel. Be sure to distribute the ingredients as evenly as possible.

4 Spread the spumoni into the plastic-lined cake pan and smooth the top with an offset spatula. Fold the ends of plastic wrap over to cover, and freeze for at least 4 hours, until completely set.

5 To serve, unwrap the spumoni and invert to unmold onto a large serving plate. Carefully peel off the plastic wrap from the top. If necessary, smooth the top of the ice cream with a spatula. Press the remaining toasted almond slices around the sides of the spumoni. Cut into wedges and serve immediately.

INGREDIENTS

⅓ cup sliced almonds

1 quart plus 1 pint (3 pints or 1½ liters) vanilla ice cream

¼ cup coarsely chopped pistachio nuts

¼ cup finely chopped bittersweet chocolate (about 1 ounce or 25 grams)

¼ cup maraschino cherries, drained with 1 tablespoon juice reserved, coarsely chopped

3 tablespoons chopped candied orange peel

Serves 8 to 10

COOL TIPS FOR SUCCESS

When serving frozen desserts, dip the knife, spoon, or scoop in hot water and quickly blot dry with a towel between each serving.

Fifty-Fifty Pops

Use any combination of sorbet and ice cream here to make your own pops.

INGREDIENTS

1   pint (450 ml) orange
    or raspberry sorbet
1   pint (450 ml) vanilla ice
    cream

Serves 8

1   Pack about ¼ cup of sorbet into 8 (4- to 5-ounce or 100- to 150-gram) plastic pop molds or paper cups, pressing firmly to remove any air pockets. If there is any sorbet left over, divide it equally among the molds, pressing down firmly. Freeze for 30 minutes, until partially frozen.

2   Pack about ¼ cup of the ice cream into the molds, packing down gently to remove any air pockets. If there is any ice cream left over, divide it equally among the molds, pressing down gently. Freeze for 30 minutes or until partially frozen.

3   Follow the package directions for inserting the plastic sticks provided, or insert a blunt wooden craft stick or a sturdy plastic spoon into the center of each cup. Freeze for 3 hours or until very firm. Unmold as the package directs; or, if using cups, tear off the paper. Serve at once, or cover with plastic wrap and store in the freezer for up to 1 week.

"the only emperor is the emperor of ice cream."

–poet Wallace Stevens

ice cream sodas, milkshakes, & floats

Cherry Soda "Manhattan" Float

Inspired by Boston chef Gabriel Frasca's brilliant creation, this grown-up float is the quintessential hybrid cocktail-dessert. Always remember that the better the quality of the bourbon and cherry soda you use, the better the finished drink will taste.

1 In a small jar with a tight-fitting lid, combine 2 tablespoons of the bourbon with the cherries. Cover and let sit at room temperature, shaking occasionally, for at least 2 hours or as long as 24 hours. Drain the cherries, reserving the bourbon.

2 In a large bowl, combine the ice cream with the remaining 6 tablespoons bourbon and the cherry juice. Using a rubber spatula or a wooden spoon, stir until well blended. Cover tightly with plastic wrap and freeze until firm, at least 2 hours. Place 4 tall glasses in the freezer or refrigerator to chill.

3 In another large bowl, combine the cream, vermouth, confectioners' sugar, and bitters. Beat with an electric mixer until soft peaks form.

4 Put 2 scoops of ice cream in each chilled glass. Top with enough soda to reach within ½ inch (1¼ cm) of the rim. Rub the cut edge of an orange peel strip over the rim of each glass and twist it over the drink to release the oils, then discard. Drizzle the reserved bourbon over each float. Top with a generous dollop of the flavored whipped cream and a cherry. Serve at once.

INGREDIENTS

½ cup bourbon whiskey

4 maraschino cherries with stems

1 quart (1 liter) Tahitian Double Vanilla Ice Cream (page 12), or your favorite premium brand, slightly softened

1 tablespoon maraschino cherry juice (from the jar of cherries)

1 cup heavy cream, chilled

1½ tablespoons sweet vermouth

1½ tablespoons confectioners' sugar

Dash of aromatic bitters, such as Angostura®

3 bottles cherry soda (12 ounces or 350 grams each), chilled

4 strips of fresh orange peel

Serves 4

Sensational
Strawberry Shake

Strawberries provide a tart undertone to offset the richness of the ice cream.

In a blender or food processor, combine the ice cream, strawberries, and milk. Process until well blended but still thick. Pour into tall, chilled glasses and serve at once.

INGREDIENTS

3   cups Almost-Instant Strawberry Ice Cream (page 20), Tahitian Double Vanilla Ice Cream (page 12), or store-bought strawberry or vanilla ice cream

1   pint (450 ml) fresh strawberries, hulled, or 1 pound (450 grams) frozen unsweetened strawberries, partially thawed

1   cup whole milk, chilled

Makes 2 large shakes

VARIATION

Very Berry Shake: Substitute a combination of 3 cups of fresh or 1 pound (450 grams) of frozen raspberries, blackberries, or blueberries for the strawberries.

...wberry Sweetheart Soda

Some people just can't get enough of the color pink. Here it is in all its glory, in a delectable soda little girls of all ages will love.

1 Place 3 tablespoons of strawberry sauce in each glass. Stir 2 tablespoons of half-and-half into each. Add 1 small scoop of ice cream; stir and mash to dissolve partially.

2 Add about ⅓ cup of seltzer to each, letting the foam rise to the top. Scoop in the remaining ice cream and top off with the remaining seltzer. Top with whipped cream and a strawberry or maraschino cherry and serve at once.

INGREDIENTS

6   tablespoons Simple Strawberry Sauce (page 112), or store-bought strawberry syrup

¼   cup half-and-half or whole milk

3   cups (1½ pints or 675 ml) Almost-Instant Strawberry Ice Cream (page 20), Tahitian Double Vanilla Ice Cream (page 12), or store-bought strawberry or vanilla ice cream

1   cup seltzer water or club soda, chilled

Whipped cream, for garnish

2   fresh strawberries or maraschino cherries, for garnish

Makes 2 large sodas

Mango Sorbet Float

Maneuvering a spoon in and out of a fragile champagne flute can be risky. Instead, serve this festive sparkling "float" in a wine glass that has a wider bowl.

Place 1 scoop of sorbet in each of 6 large, chilled wine glasses. Pour about ¾ cup of the Prosecco in each and serve at once.

INGREDIENTS

1½ pints (675 ml) Mango-
     Pineapple Sorbet (page
     88), or store-bought
     mango sorbet

1   bottle (750 ml) Prosecco
     or other dry but fruity
     sparkling wine

Serves 6

VARIATION

Mango-Raspberry Float: Put a small scoop of mango sorbet and a small scoop of raspberry sorbet into 6 to 8 tall glasses. Divide a bottle (750 ml) of Prosecco among the glasses. Garnish each with a few raspberries, if you have them.

Lemon Vodka Martini Shake

Get a head start on summer entertaining by stashing a batch or two of this refreshing cocktail in your freezer. Pour into freezer-safe martini glasses (not your best crystal) or plastic tumblers and—voila!—drinks are ready when the guests arrive. Because of the alcohol content, these remain seductively soft and slushy in the freezer. As summer goes on, you may wish to vary the flavor of sorbet and vodka—raspberry makes a strikingly beautiful (and delicious) shake.

In a blender or food processor, combine the sorbet, ice, vodka, and lemon juice. Process just until blended. Pour into plastic glasses and serve at once, or cover each glass tightly with plastic wrap and freeze for up to 1 week. To serve, garnish each with a lemon twist, if desired.

INGREDIENTS

1   pint (450 ml) Meyer Lemon Sorbet (page 84), or store-bought lemon sorbet

1½ cups crushed ice

1   cup chilled lemon-flavored or plain vodka, or more to taste

6   tablespoons fresh lemon juice

Lemon twists

Serves 6 to 8

Lime-in-the-Coconut Shake

One sip and you'll be transported to a warm beach, wiggling your toes in the sand and listening to the sounds of a steel drum band in the distance. At your fantasy island resort, this would probably be served in a coconut shell with a paper parasol and all the other fancy accoutrements, but back in the real world that seems like overkill for such an easily made beverage. Don't try to cut corners by omitting the toasted coconut—it ties together all of the flavors.

1 Preheat the oven to 350°F (180°C). Spread out the coconut evenly in a small shallow pan. Toast in the oven, stirring frequently, for 7 to 10 minutes, or until lightly browned. Set aside to cool.

2 In a blender or food processor, combine the ice cream, coconut milk, and limeade concentrate. Process until well blended but still thick.

3 Divide among 4 tall, chilled glasses. Top each with a dollop of whipped cream and 2 tablespoons of toasted coconut. Garnish with a slice of lime and serve at once.

INGREDIENTS

½ cup sweetened flaked coconut

3 cups Tahitian Double Vanilla Ice Cream (page 12), or store-bought vanilla ice cream or frozen yogurt

1 can (about 14 ounces or 400 grams) light or regular coconut milk, chilled and well shaken

½ cup frozen limeade concentrate

Whipped cream, for garnish

4 lime slices, for garnish

Makes 4 servings

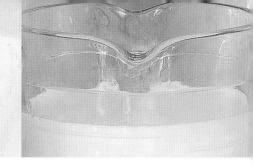

California Date Shake

Ranchers in the southern California desert grow over 99 percent of the dates sold in America. Due to the accessibility of this local crop, many restaurants and soda fountains in nearby towns tempt travelers with highway billboards advertising ice cold date shakes as relief for parched palates. The chewy bits of date scattered throughout the creamy shake make for an interesting textural contrast, as well as an exceptional burst of flavor.

In a blender or food processor, combine the dates and milk. Process until the dates are finely chopped. Add the ice cream and vanilla and process until well blended but still thick. Pour into tall, chilled glasses and serve at once.

INGREDIENTS

1   cup whole pitted dates

1   cup whole milk, chilled

3   cups (1½ pints or 675 ml) Tahitian Double Vanilla Ice Cream (page 12), or store-bought vanilla ice cream

½   teaspoon vanilla extract

Makes 2 large servings

VARIATION

Banana-Date Shake: In a blender or food processor, combine 1 ripe banana with ½ cup of whole pitted dates. Process until the dates are finely chopped. Add the ice cream and milk and process until well blended but still thick. Pour into tall, chilled glasses and serve at once.

Ice Cream
with Spiked Espresso

Long before espresso entered the American coffee vocabulary, savvy Italians made *affogato* by "drowning" gelato in hot espresso. For a seriously adult dessert, take this excellent idea one step further by adding a generous splash of your favorite liqueur. (And a puffy cloud of whipped cream never hurts, either.)

1 Divide the ice cream among 4 heatproof glasses, coffee cups, or bowls. (This can be done several hours in advance and kept covered in the freezer.)

2 Just before serving, pour ¼ cup hot espresso and 2 tablespoons of the liqueur over each portion of ice cream. Top with whipped cream and hazelnuts, if desired. Serve at once.

INGREDIENTS

1   pint (450 ml) vanilla or coffee gelato

1   cup hot, freshly brewed espresso or strong coffee (regular or decaf)

½   cup hazelnut liqueur, such as Frangelico®, coffee liqueur, dark rum, or brandy

Whipped cream and/or chopped toasted hazelnuts, for garnish

Serves 4

Macchiato Milkshake

Macchiato literally means dotted, which here translates to foamed milk on top of espresso—as well as an irresistibly elegant shake.

In a blender or food processor, combine the ice cream, milk, and espresso. Process until well blended but still thick. Pour into tall, chilled glasses and serve at once.

INGREDIENTS

1   quart (1 liter) Coffee Ice Cream (page 32), or your favorite premium brand

¾   cup whole milk

¾   cup brewed espresso or strong coffee, chilled

Makes 2 large shakes

VARIATION

Macchiato-Kahlúa Milkshake: In a blender or food processor, combine the ice cream, milk, and espresso as directed above. Add ¼ cup Kahlúa or other coffee-flavored liqueur. Process until well blended but still thick. Pour into tall, chilled glasses and serve at once.

Black and White Ice Cream Soda

This all-time classic soda gets its name from the "black" chocolate syrup and the "white" vanilla ice cream. However you refer to it, it remains one of the greatest ice cream drinks ever invented.

1 Place 3 tablespoons of chocolate syrup in each glass. Stir in 2 tablespoons of half-and-half. Add 1 small scoop of ice cream, stirring and mashing to blend.

2 Pour about ⅓ cup of seltzer into each, letting foam rise to the top. Scoop in the remaining ice cream and top off with the remaining seltzer. Top with whipped cream and a cherry and serve at once.

Chocolate Syrup

1 In a medium saucepan, combine the sugar, cocoa powder, and salt. Gradually whisk in the water until smooth.

2 Bring to a boil over medium heat, stirring to dissolve the sugar. Cook for 3 minutes longer, stirring constantly. Remove from the heat and let cool. Stir in the vanilla. Serve at once, or refrigerate, covered, for up to 1 week.

INGREDIENTS

6 tablespoons Chocolate Syrup (recipe follows), or your favorite brand

¼ cup half-and-half or whole milk

4 scoops of Tahitian Double Vanilla Ice Cream (page 12), or your favorite premium brand

1 cup seltzer water or club soda, chilled

Whipped cream, for garnish

2 maraschino cherries, for garnish

Makes 2 large shakes

Chocolate Syrup

1 cup sugar

½ cup Dutch process unsweetened cocoa powder

Dash of salt

1 cup water

1 teaspoon vanilla extract

Makes about 1¾ cups

Chocolate Mini-Malts with Pound Cake "Fries"

Sometimes it's fun to end a dinner party with a whimsical dessert, especially if it tastes as clever as it looks. Although most of us would never consider ordering a huge milkshake after dinner, a small juice glass containing just a few sips is a reasonable indulgence. And to round out the nostalgic feeling, a side order of "fries" is added to the plate. You could even give each guest a tablespoon or two of Simple Strawberry Sauce (page 170) as "ketchup" for their fries.

1 Preheat the oven to 325°F (160°C). Slice off the rounded top of the cake, as well as the dark outer crust on the bottom and sides of the loaf. Cut the cake in half crosswise; then cut each half horizontally into 3 slices about ½ inch (1¼ cm) thick. Working with half of the cake at a time, stack the layers and cut into strips about ½ inch wide and 3½ inches long (1¼ cm wide by 8¾ cm long) to resemble french fries.

2 Arrange the "fries" in a single layer on a parchment- or foil-lined baking sheet. Brush with the melted butter. Bake for about 7 minutes, until lightly browned around the edges.

3 Meanwhile, in a blender or food processor, combine the ice cream, milk, chocolate syrup, malted milk powder, and vanilla. Process until well blended but still thick. Divide among 8 small chilled glasses. Place 1 mini shake on each dessert plate, with several warm "fries" on the side. Serve at once.

INGREDIENTS

1   frozen all-butter pound cake (10¾ ounces or 290 grams), thawed

3   tablespoons unsalted butter, melted

1   pint (450 ml) Tahitian Double Vanilla Ice Cream (page 12), Chocolate Custard Ice Cream (page 30), or store-bought vanilla or chocolate ice cream

1   cup whole milk, chilled

3   tablespoons Chocolate Syrup (page 179), or store-bought chocolate syrup

3   tablespoons malted milk powder

½   teaspoon vanilla extract

Makes 8 (4-ounce or 100-gram) servings

Root Beer Float

In this world of snazzy coffee drinks, it's easy to overlook something as old-fashioned as the "brown cow." There are a number of artisans now producing very high-quality root beers; and when paired with homemade ice cream, it's hard to think of a more delectable combination.

Pour about ¼ cup of root beer into the bottoms of 4 tall chilled glasses. Add a large scoop of ice cream to each, mashing with a spoon to form a thick liquid. Add a second scoop of ice cream. Fill the glasses with the remaining root beer and serve at once.

INGREDIENTS

2   bottles (12 ounces or 350 grams each) root beer

1   pint (450 ml) Tahitian Double Vanilla Ice Cream (page 12), or your favorite premium brand

Makes 4 large floats

VARIATIONS

Black Cow: Substitute cola for the root beer.

Ginger Float: Substitute ginger ale for the root beer.

Vanilla Shake

For those who love vanilla, the simpler the better. Here's an old-fashioned shake that doesn't rock the boat.

In a blender or food processor, combine the ice cream, milk, and vanilla. Process until well blended but still thick. Pour into tall, chilled glasses and serve at once.

INGREDIENTS

1   quart (1 liter) Tahitian Double Vanilla Ice Cream (page 12), or your favorite premium brand

1½ cups whole milk, chilled

1   teaspoon vanilla extract

Makes 2 large shakes

Coffee Shake
(see Variation below)

1   quart (1 liter) Coffee Ice Cream (page 32), or store-bought coffee ice cream

1½ cups cold brewed coffee

1   tablespoon Kahlúa or 1 teaspoon vanilla extract

Makes 2 large shakes

VARIATION

Coffee Shake: In a blender or food processor, combine the coffee ice cream, coffee, and Kahlúa or vanilla. Process until well blended but still thick. Pour into tall, chilled glasses and serve at once.

Sauces, Toppings, & Pie Shells

Bittersweet Fudge Sauce

1 cup heavy cream
2 tablespoons light
   corn syrup
Dash of salt

8 ounces (225 grams)
bittersweet chocolate, finely
chopped

1 teaspoon vanilla extract
   or 1 tablespoon cognac,
   Kahlúa, or Grand Marnier

In a heavy medium saucepan, combine the cream, corn syrup, and salt. Bring to a boil over medium heat, whisking frequently, until well blended. Remove from the heat. Add the chocolate and whisk until melted and smooth. Let the sauce cool for 10 to 15 minutes. Stir in the vanilla and use at once, or refrigerate, covered, for up to 1 week. Serve warm or at room temperature.

Makes about 1½ cups

Chocolate-Nut Sauce

¾ cup whole blanched
   almonds, or pecan
   or walnut pieces,
   or roasted peanuts

12 ounces (350 grams)
semisweet chocolate, finely
chopped

Dash of salt

Preheat the oven to 350°F

(180°C). If using peanuts, skip to the next step. Spread out the nuts in a small baking pan. Toast in the oven for 7 to 10 minutes, stirring once or twice, until lightly browned and fragrant. Transfer to a dish and let cool, then chop coarsely. Place a heatproof bowl over a pot of barely simmering water. Add the chocolate and cook over low heat, stirring, until melted and smooth. Stir in the nuts and salt. Serve warm.

Makes about 1½ cups

Chocolate Ganache

1 cup heavy cream
Dash of salt
8 ounces (225 grams)
bittersweet or semisweet
chocolate, finely chopped

In a small saucepan, combine the cream and salt. Bring to a boil over medium heat. Remove from the heat and add the chopped chocolate; stir until melted and smooth. Let cool until the sauce is fluid but not thin. If made in advance, refrigerate for up to 1 week. Reheat gently before serving.

Makes about 1½ cups

Easy Chocolate Sauce

¾ cup sugar
¼ cup light corn syrup
½ cup warm water
Dash of salt
4 ounces (100 grams)
bittersweet chocolate, finely
chopped
½ teaspoon vanilla extract

In a medium saucepan, combine the sugar, corn syrup, ¼ cup of the warm water, and the salt. Bring to a boil over medium-high heat. Reduce the heat to low and stir for 1 minute or until sugar dissolves. Remove from the heat and add the chocolate; stir until melted and smooth. Set aside for 10 minutes. Stir in the vanilla and the remaining ¼ cup warm water. Serve at once, or cover and refrigerate for up to 1 week. Serve slightly warm.

Makes about 1½ cups

Mocha Fudge Sauce

1 cup (6 ounces or 175 grams)
   semisweet chocolate chips
¾ cup heavy cream
1 tablespoon instant
   coffee crystals
Dash of salt
¼ cup light corn syrup

Place the chocolate chips in

a bowl and set aside. In a medium saucepan, combine the cream, coffee crystals, and salt. Cook, stirring, until the coffee is dissolved and the liquid is barely simmering. Stir in the corn syrup and remove from the heat. Immediately pour the warm coffee cream over the chocolate chips. Let stand for 2 minutes, then whisk until melted and smooth. Use at once or let cool to room temperature, then cover and refrigerate for up to 1 week. To serve, reheat the sauce gently in the top of a double boiler or in the microwave.

Makes about 1½ cups

Chocolate Whipped Cream

6   tablespoons unsweetened cocoa powder
6   tablespoons granulated sugar
1   cup heavy cream

Sift the cocoa and sugar through a fine sieve placed over a large bowl. Gradually whisk in the cream until blended. Cover and refrigerate for at least 30 minutes to dissolve the sugar and cocoa. Beat with an electric mixer until soft peaks form. (This mixture whips up very quickly, so be careful not to overbeat.) Use at once or cover and refrigerate

for up to 2 hours.

Makes about 2 cups

Toffee Sauce

1½ sticks (6 ounces or 175 grams) unsalted butter, cut into pieces
1½ cups (packed) dark brown sugar
¾   cup heavy cream
Dash of salt
1½ teaspoons vanilla extract or 1½ tablespoons brandy

In a heavy medium saucepan, combine the butter, brown sugar, cream, and salt. Bring to a boil over medium-high heat, stirring constantly with a wooden spoon. Remove from the heat and let cool for 10 minutes. Stir the vanilla into the warm toffee sauce. Serve at once, or refrigerate, covered, for up to 1 week. Reheat gently before serving.

Makes about 2 cups

Caramel Sauce

1   stick (4 ounces or 100 grams) unsalted butter, cut into pieces
1   cup sugar
Dash of salt
1   cup heavy cream, at room temperature

In a heavy 1-quart (1-liter) saucepan, melt the butter over medium heat. Stir in the sugar and salt. Cook until the caramel turns a medium amber

color. (Don't worry if the butter and sugar separate or become grainy at this point; they will come together later.) Remove the pan from the heat and slowly whisk in the cream. Let the sauce cool to room temperature, then cover and refrigerate. Serve chilled or at room temperature.

If made more than a few hours in advance, transfer to a glass jar with a tight-fitting lid and refrigerate for up to 1 week.

Makes about 2 cups

Caramel Banana-Rum Sauce

⅔   cup (packed) brown sugar
⅔   cup dark rum, such as Myers's
4   tablespoons unsalted butter, cut into pieces
⅛   teaspoon ground cinnamon
⅛   teaspoon freshly grated nutmeg
¼   cup heavy cream
3   large firm but ripe bananas

Combine the brown sugar and rum in a heavy nonreactive 1-quart (1-liter) saucepan. Cook over medium-high heat, stirring often, for 4 to 5 minutes, or until the sugar melts, large bubbles appear on the surface, and the mixture has thickened. Reduce the heat to medium and add the butter. Stir frequently, until the butter has melted. Stir in the cinnamon and nutmeg. Carefully stir in the cream, 1 tablespoon at a time. Cut the bananas crosswise into ¼-inch (⅝-cm) thick slices and add them to the sauce, stirring gently to coat. Reduce heat to low and simmer until the bananas are slightly cooked but hold their shape. Remove the sauce from the heat and let cool for 5 to 10 minutes before spooning over each serving.

Makes about 2 cups

Maple-Bathed Walnuts

1 cup walnut pieces
¼ cup maple syrup
¼ cup light corn syrup

Preheat the oven to 350°F (180°C). Spread out the walnuts evenly in a baking pan. Toast in the oven for 8 to 10 minutes, stirring once or twice, until lightly browned and fragrant. Transfer to a dish and set aside to cool. In a medium bowl, combine the toasted walnuts, maple syrup, and corn syrup. Stir until the nuts are well coated. Store in a covered jar in the refrigerator.

Makes about 1 cup

Shortbread Pastry Shell

1 cup all-purpose flour
2 tablespoons sugar
⅛ teaspoon salt
1 stick (4 ounces or 100 grams) cold unsalted butter, cut into 8 pieces

Preheat the oven to 375°F (190°C). Lightly coat a 9-inch (23-cm) tart pan with a removable bottom with nonstick cooking spray. Set the tart pan on a baking sheet. In a food processor, combine the flour, sugar, and salt. Process briefly to blend. Add the butter and pulse until the mixture forms coarse crumbs and begins to hold together. Turn out the dough and knead a few times until smooth. Press the dough evenly onto the bottom and up the sides of the tart pan. Bake for 15 to 18 minutes, until the crust is light golden. Transfer the tart pan to a wire rack and cool completely. Then gently remove the sides of the pan, leaving the shell on the metal bottom.

Makes 1 (9-inch or 23-cm) tart shell

Graham Cracker Crumb Crust

1½ cups graham cracker crumbs, about 30 (2-inch or 5-cm square) graham crackers
2 tablespoons sugar
6 tablespoons unsalted butter, melted

Preheat the oven to 325°F (160°C) . In a medium bowl, mix together the cookie crumbs and sugar until well blended. Add the butter, stirring to moisten the crumbs evenly. Press the mixture evenly over the bottom and up the sides of a 9-inch (23-cm) pie pan, building the crumbs up slightly to form a small ridge above the rim of the pan. Bake the pie shell for 10 minutes. Let cool completely, then chill the crust in the freezer for at least 15 minutes before filling it with ice cream.

Makes 1 (9-inch or 23-cm) pie shell

Gingersnap Crumb Crust

1½ cups gingersnap cookie crumbs
2 tablespoons sugar
6 tablespoons unsalted butter, melted

Preheat the oven to 325°F (160°C). In a medium bowl, mix together the cookie crumbs and sugar until well blended. Add the butter, stirring to moisten all of the crumbs. Press the mixture evenly over the bottom and up the sides of a 9-inch (23-cm) pie pan, building the crumbs up slightly to form a small ridge above the rim of the pan.

Bake the gingersnap crumb crust for 10 minutes. Let cool completely, then chill the crust in the freezer for at least 15 minutes before filling it with ice cream.

Makes 1 (9-inch or 23-cm) pie shell

Chocolate Crumb Crust

2   cups chocolate wafer cookie crumbs (about 35 chocolate wafer cookies, such as Nabisco® Famous Chocolate Wafers)

2   tablespoons sugar

6   tablespoons unsalted butter, melted

Preheat the oven to 325°F (160°C). In a medium bowl, mix together the cookie crumbs and sugar until well blended. Add the butter, stirring to moisten all of the crumbs. Press the mixture over the bottom and up the sides of a 9-inch (23-cm) pie pan, building the crumbs up slightly to form a small ridge above the rim. Bake for 10 minutes. Cool completely, then chill the crust in the freezer for 15 minutes before filling it with ice cream.

Makes 1 (9-inch or 23-cm) pie shell

Chocolate Curls

1   large bar or piece (at least 4 ounces or 100 grams) milk chocolate, semisweet, bittersweet, or white chocolate, at warm room temperature

Use a paper towel to hold the chocolate by its edge so the heat from your fingers doesn't melt it. Working over a baking sheet lined with waxed paper, use a swivel-bladed vegetable peeler to gently press against the edges of the chocolate bar and "peel" away curls. Let the curls fall onto the waxed paper. Avoid touching the chocolate, as the heat from your hands could be enough to melt the curls. Refrigerate or freeze the baking sheet for 15 minutes, or until the chocolate curls are firm to the touch. Cover with plastic wrap or, working quickly, use a metal spatula to carefully transfer the curls to an airtight container. Refrigerate or freeze until needed.

To serve, use a metal spatula to lift the cold chocolate curls from the waxed paper and place them on the ice cream.

Makes enough to garnish 4 to 6 servings

Brandied Fruit Sauce

1   orange

1   lemon

2   Granny Smith or other tart green apples, peeled, seeded, and chopped

¾   cup apple cider or unsweetened juice

½   cup chopped pitted dates

½   cup golden raisins (sultanas)

⅓   cup bourbon, brandy, or dark rum

¼   cup dried currants

¼   cup finely chopped candied angelica, pineapple, or lemon peel

¼   cup (packed) brown sugar

¼   cup water

2   tablespoons cider vinegar

2   tablespoons unsalted butter

½   teaspoon ground cinnamon

⅛   teaspoon grated nutmeg

⅛   teaspoon ground cardamom

Grate the zest from half the orange and half the lemon. Squeeze out the juice from both whole fruit. Combine the zest and juice with all of the other ingredients in a nonreactive large saucepan. Bring to a boil, partially cover, and cook over medium heat, stirring occasionally, for 15 to 20 minutes, or until the apples are tender and the sauce has thickened. Let cool; then cover and refrigerate.

Makes about 2 cups

Frozen dessert glossary

The vast variety of frozen desserts is one of the pleasures of homemade. In this book, whether a frozen dessert is technically an ice cream, a frozen custard, or a light ice cream is somewhat arbitrary, though the designation does give you an idea of the fat content and richness. Here are how the terms are defined:

Ice Cream: Generally designated by its higher concentration of butterfat (i.e., cream), ice cream comes in two varieties: "Philadelphia-style" ice creams do not contain eggs; custard-style ice creams, which most resemble commercially made super-premium brands, are made from a cooked egg-custard base.

Frozen Custard: Ice cream made with an egg yolk-custard base. Many frozen custards are simply called "ice cream."

Gelato: Synonymous with Italian ice cream, gelato traditionally contains only a small amount of butterfat. Commercially made gelato has less air churned into it than ice cream, giving it a denser texture. Gelato may or may not contain eggs.

Light Ice Cream: Containing milk products other than cream—usually half-and-half—light ice cream is richer than ice milk, but less rich than ice cream.

Ice Milk: Ice milk contains no cream, which makes it lower in fat. It is often served softer than ice cream, as it has a tendency to become icy when frozen solid. Ice milks are best eaten within a day or two.

Sherbet: An eggless ice mixture of fruit and milk or cream, churned along with sugar and other flavorings.

Sorbet: An ice generally made without dairy products. It is usually fruit based, but chocolate and coffee are also popular flavors.

Ice (sometimes called *Italian Ice*): The American version of granita. Most popular in the Northeast, ices are often served in paper cups. Primarily made from syrups or other liquids, or sometimes fruit, its texture is smoother than a Snow Cone but not as granular as a granita.

Granita: An Italian ice that derives its fluffy, granular texture from repeated stirring and scraping as it freezes.

Frozen Yogurt: Very similar to ice cream in texture, frozen yogurt is far lower in calories. Yogurt has a rich, slightly acidic taste that pairs particularly well with fruit.

Frozen Soy Milk: Offering a healthful alternative for people with special dietary needs, frozen soy milk provides a very satisfactory substitute for cow's milk when combined with flavorings.

Index

Page numbers in *italics* refer to photographs.

Author's Acknowledgments

A heartfelt month of sundaes go to fellow food professionals who generously contributed their recipe development and testing skills to this book: Karen Baxter, John Carroll, Linda Gollober, Beth Hensperger, Joyce Jue, Rosemary Mark, Michelle Schmidt, and Barbara Shenson.

Sweet recognition also goes to "international correspondents" Gary Doherty, David Pantalena, and Gabrielle Saylor who promptly answered all of my late-night emails with wisdom and good humor.

A double-dip thank you to Rachel Litner, Mary Rodgers, Ilona Gollinger and Cuisinart, and to Lello Appliances for providing ice cream machines for testing and photography.

Cherry-topped kudos to Susan Wyler, who once again condensed my ramblings into readable prose.

And to Nichole Morford at DK Publishing, a flurry of thanks for staying cool while making split decisions.